S0-AWH-931

Endorsements for *By Grace Alone*

"This is a beautiful book—a providential confluence of two pastors' hearts (separated by time and culture) on the theme of grace. First, there is the pulsing heart of an obscure African pastor, Emmanuel T. Sibomana, who, many years ago, penned the magnificent seven-stanza hymn 'O How the Grace of God Amazes Me.' Then there is the grateful and responsive heart of well-known pastor-theologian Sinclair Ferguson, who has taken the seven dazzling facets of the African hymn and held them up to the manifold light of God's Word so that they further grace and enlighten our souls. *By Grace Alone* is a book that will fire your heart."

—R. Kent Hughes
Senior pastor emeritus, College Church
Wheaton, Illinois

"Most of us have books lying on a table or bookshelf somewhere, waiting for us to get around to reading them. Please don't let this book be in that category. Sinclair Ferguson is one of the clearest, brightest lights in evangelical Christianity today. This book will point you to the freedom and exuberance of living in the grace of God through Jesus Christ. Read this book for your own encouragement, and pass it along to a new disciple or an (as yet) unbelieving neighbor."

—Russell D. Moore
Dean, School of Theology
Vice president for academic administration
The Southern Baptist Theological Seminary
Louisville, Kentucky

"Rich in biblical exposition and in theological depth, *By Grace Alone* is a series of great messages by one of today's greatest preachers on some of the greatest Scripture texts—all on one of the greatest themes of the Bible: *amazing grace!* This book will excite your mind, stir your affection, convict your soul, win your heart, and move you to action. It will evangelize, disciple, and mature all kinds of readers. Dr. Ferguson has given us another feast, and there is food here for all—saved and unsaved, ministers and laypeople, young and old."

—*Joel R. Beeke*
President, Puritan Reformed Theological Seminary
Grand Rapids, Michigan

"Sinclair Ferguson's biblically insightful and pastorally profound meditations on the manifold grace of God are strung like pearls on the stanzas of the African hymn 'O How the Grace of God Amazes Me.' Christ is at the very center, as He must be: in Him, our enslaved hearts find freedom, our guilty hearts find forgiveness, our troubled hearts find a Defender in the darkness, and our embattled hearts find strength to resist the enemy's enticements. Thirsty hearts, come to Jesus and drink deeply from His fountain of amazing, life-giving, joy-imparting, hope-sustaining grace."

—*Dennis E. Johnson*
Professor of practical theology, Westminster Seminary California
Escondido, California

BY GRACE
ALONE

SINCLAIR B. FERGUSON

BY GRACE ALONE

HOW THE GRACE OF GOD AMAZES ME

ℝ

Reformation Trust

PUBLISHING

A DIVISION OF LIGONIER MINISTRIES · ORLANDO, FLORIDA

By Grace Alone: How the Grace of God Amazes Me

© 2010 by Sinclair B. Ferguson

Published by Reformation Trust Publishing
a division of Ligonier Ministries
400 Technology Park, Lake Mary, FL 32746
www.ligonier.org   www.reformationtrust.com

Printed in Harrisonburg, Virginia
RR Donnelley and Sons
March 2011
First edition, second printing

All rights reserved. No part of this publication may be reproduced, stored in a retrieval system, or transmitted in any form or by any means—electronic, mechanical, photocopy, recording, or otherwise—without the prior written permission of the publisher, Reformation Trust Publishing. The only exception is brief quotations in printed reviews.

Creative direction: Geoff Stevens
Cover design: Faceout Studio
Interior design and typeset: Katherine Lloyd, The DESK

Unless otherwise indicated, all Scripture quotations are from the *New King James Version*®. Copyright © 1982 by Thomas Nelson. Used by permission. All rights reserved.

Scripture quotations marked ESV are from The Holy Bible, *English Standard Version*, copyright © 2001 by Crossway Bibles, a division of Good News Publishers. Used by permission. All rights reserved.

Scripture quotations marked NIV are from The Holy Bible, *New International Version*®. NIV®. Copyright © 1973, 1978, 1984 by International Bible Society. Used by permission of Zondervan. All rights reserved.

The hymn "O How the Grace of God Amazes Me" (words by Emmanuel T. Sibomana, music by Frederick John Barff), quoted throughout the book, is copyright Church Mission Society. Used by permission. All rights reserved.

Library of Congress Cataloging-in-Publication Data

Ferguson, Sinclair B.
  By grace alone : how the grace of God amazes me / Sinclair B. Ferguson.
     p. cm.
  Includes bibliographical references and index.
  ISBN 978-1-56769-202-0
  1. Grace (Theology) 2. Sibomana, Emmanuel T. O how the grace of God amazes me. I. Title.
  BT761.3.F47 2010
  234--dc22

                                        2009048999

To
Murdo and Alison
Maclean

Once colleagues, always friends
With gratitude and affection

CONTENTS

FOREWORD

I met Sinclair Ferguson in July 2009 in Geneva, Switzerland, as a number of church leaders came together to celebrate the five-hundredth anniversary of the birth of John Calvin, one of the renowned European Reformers and a preacher of divine grace. When Sinclair asked me to write the foreword for this book, I did not know what a surprise the grace of God had in store for me.

One midmorning on a Wednesday in September of this year, I went to visit a home in a suburb of Kampala City, Uganda. This is not an ordinary home, but a home that brings in orphans and needy children from the streets and offers the love of Jesus to them. We were met by about thirty smiling children whose faces were happy, healthy, and confident. Then they began to tell me their stories. One little girl had been picked up by the police when she was only three weeks old, abandoned and rejected. Another had been found out in the cold without food, shelter, or clothing. The stories continued on and on.

The children told us their stories in a song composed by the director of this ministry. This song was sad yet joyful, pessimistic yet with a note of victory. As I listened, the words and the melody undressed my dignified posture. I melted in my heart.

One of the children, a thirteen-year-old girl named Ana (not her real name), caught my attention. The Holy Spirit highlighted her face as I watched her singing. She looked beautiful, yet there was a trace of sadness in her face. She had lost both parents at an early age and had struggled alone in the streets of Kampala before arriving at this home of transition.

I knew this young girl would haunt me for the rest of my life if I did not respond to her. Two weeks after this encounter, Ana became part of my family.

In his book, Sinclair reveals the amazing surprises of God that we call "grace." He shows us how God stoops low to reach a longing lost soul, a soul that has walked a path of loneliness and darkness, a soul that, like Ana, would never consider that a change was possible. God comes because He watches with great love and moves with unspeakable tenderness. His desire is to rescue the broken and the bleeding, the lost and the lonely.

Sinclair provides a glimpse of this grace to the inquisitive mind and hungry soul. I commend his book to the one who is longing to know the truth of God searching for us. Your soul will be nourished and your faith strengthened.

—*The Most Rev. Henry Luke Orombi*
Archbishop, (Anglican) Church of Uganda
Kampala, Uganda
October 2009

PREFACE

The inspiration behind these pages is the remarkable hymn written by an African pastor, Emmanuel T. Sibomana. He was born around 1915 and lived near Musema, a Baptist mission in central Burundi. He became a Christian in his late teens or his early twenties, and later became a Baptist pastor. Then, in 1946, he published a hymn titled "*Umbuntu Bg Imana*." Pastor Sibomana's hymn was translated by an English missionary in Rwanda, Rosemary Guillebaud, as "O How the Grace of God Amazes Me."

The hymn captures the rich contours and multisided character of the grace of God. Its easily sung tune, *Grace of God*, has often brought its words to my mind unprompted. Reflecting on the themes of its verses led me eventually to work through the biblical material that lies behind them. This book is the result.

Although different in format—the chapters are fewer but longer—*By Grace Alone* is a companion volume to *In Christ Alone: Living the Gospel-Centered Life* (Reformation Trust, 2007). These are among the great watchwords of biblical teaching and capture two great emphases in historical evangelical theology.

But why yet another book on the grace of God? Because, as Pastor Sibomana's hymn reminds us, "the grace of God amazes me." We can never reflect too much on God's grace.

That theme is by no means unique to this particular hymn. The converted slave-trader John Newton's most famous hymn, of course, opens with the words, "Amazing grace!— how sweet the sound—that saved a wretch like me!"[1] The great English hymn writers Isaac Watts and Charles Wesley also wrote on this theme. Watts reflected on "Love so amazing, so divine."[2] Wesley, who seems to have written virtually a hymn a day in his spare time, taught the church to sing the words: "Amazing love! How can it be that thou, my God, should'st die for me?"[3] Much later, Charles H. Gabriel confessed, "I stand amazed in the presence of Jesus the Nazarene."[4]

Still, why a book on "How the grace of God *amazes* me"? For one reason: not all Christians find it so amazing.

Being amazed by God's grace is a sign of spiritual vitality. It is a litmus test of how firm and real is our grasp of the Christian gospel and how close is our walk with Jesus Christ. The growing Christian finds that the grace of God astonishes and amazes.

Yet we frequently take the grace of God for granted. We think: "*Of course* God is gracious." Or: "*Of course* we deserve His grace. After all, are we not His people?" We may never say these things. But when we think like this, the grace of God ceases to be amazing. Sadly, it also ceases to be grace.

A chief reason for the weakness of the Christian church in the West, for the poverty of our witness and any lack of vitality in our worship, probably lies here: we sing about "amazing grace" and speak of "amazing grace," but far too often it has ceased to amaze us. Sadly, we might more truthfully sing of "accustomed grace." We have lost the joy and energy that are experienced when grace seems truly amazing.

With the help of Pastor Sibomana's hymn, these pages reflect on God's grace from seven angles. Tasting the power of the grace of God can refresh the inner sanctuaries of our being, and banish the spiritual lethargy and indifference that take God's goodness and love for granted. After all, if we are not amazed by God's grace, can we really be living in it? By its very nature, God's grace astonishes those who taste it and amazes those who receive it.

I am thankful for those who have encouraged me to prepare these studies for publication.

Eve Huffman, my secretary at First Presbyterian Church, Columbia, has again given her characteristically efficient and willing help in this task. I am also deeply grateful to our elders and deacons, and to our congregation, for the encouragement they give their team of pastors to keep going in the work of the ministry.

Greg Bailey has once again served me as editor, friend, and literary Barnabas, and I want to express to him my real sense of appreciation for his ongoing help.

By Grace Alone celebrates the gospel by means of a hymn of the church in Africa. I am especially grateful, therefore, to Henry Orombi, archbishop of the Church of Uganda, for contributing the foreword. When Reformation Trust suggested the possibility of an African Christian doing this, Archbishop Orombi's name came immediately to mind. He is a kindred spirit to all men and women of grace, as I discovered one memorable Sunday when we shared the privilege of preaching in John Calvin's pulpit in the Cathedral Church of St. Peter in Geneva, Switzerland. In Calvin's day, the message of gospel grace spread throughout the Northern Hemisphere and to the West; today, it spreads like a flood throughout the Southern Hemisphere and to the East. Now North and South, East and West can rejoice together in the way grace reigns in many hearts among the nations. Truly "how the grace of God amazes me!"

My wife, Dorothy, and, with her, our whole family continue to provide a world of love and devotion that surrounds and supports me in ministry. Again, I want to express my own love and thanks for the sacrifices they have made over many years, and my gratitude for God's grace in their lives and families.

Grace is not a "thing." It is not a substance that can be measured or a commodity to be distributed. It is "the grace of the Lord Jesus Christ" (2 Cor. 13:14). In essence, it is Jesus Himself. For that reason alone, there surely could be no better companion volume to *In Christ Alone* than *By Grace Alone*.

—*Sinclair B. Ferguson*
The First Presbyterian Church
Columbia, South Carolina
September 2009

"O How the Grace of God Amazes Me"

O how the grace of God
Amazes me!
It loosed me from my bonds
And set me free!
What made it happen so?
His own will, this much I know,
Set me, as now I show,
At liberty.

My God has chosen me,
Though one of nought,
To sit beside my King
In heaven's court.
Hear what my Lord has done
O, the love that made him run
To meet his erring son!
This has God wrought.

Not for my righteousness,
For I have none,
But for his mercy's sake,
Jesus, God's Son,
Suffered on Calvary's tree—
Crucified with thieves was he—
Great was his grace to me,
His wayward one.

And when I think of how,
At Calvary,
He bore sin's penalty
Instead of me,
Amazed, I wonder why
He, the sinless One, should die
For one so vile as I;
My Saviour he!

Now all my heart's desire
Is to abide
In him, my Saviour dear,
In him to hide.
My shield and buckler he,
Covering and protecting me;
From Satan's darts I'll be
Safe at his side.

Lord Jesus, hear my prayer,
Your grace impart;
When evil thoughts arise
Through Satan's art,
O, drive them all away
And do you, from day to day,
Keep me beneath your sway,
King of my heart.

Come now, the whole of me,
Eyes, ears, and voice.
Join me, creation all,
With joyful noise:
Praise him who broke the chain
Holding me in sin's domain
And set me free again!
Sing and rejoice!

—EMMANUEL T. SIBOMANA

1

O how the grace of God
Amazes me!
It loosed me from my bonds
And set me free!
What made it happen so?
His own will, this much I know,
Set me, as now I show,
At liberty.

Chapter One

MY CHAINS FELL OFF

Grace "loosed me from my bonds and set me free!"

These simple words express the experience of the typical Christian, in every place, age, and language.

The grace of God in Jesus Christ brings freedom. To experience this grace is liberation. Our chains, shackles, burdens—describe them how we will—are broken. We are delivered from a guilty conscience. We come to trust in Christ and are immediately released. Then we progressively enjoy that freedom. We are no longer in bondage. Instead, we are free men and women in Jesus Christ.

E. T. Sibomana begins his hymn "O How the Grace of God Amazes Me" at the point of personal experience.

Of course, our experience is not actually where the grace of God itself begins. It goes back much farther than our individual experience of it. But this hymn begins with our experience because this is where we take our first conscious steps into the sea of grace. Then we discover that it is in fact a boundless ocean that seems to have no bottom. As we sink into it, we begin to realize that its origins lie in God Himself in eternity.

This is the grace that "loosed me from my bonds."

His own will, this much I know,
Set me, as now I show,
At liberty.

Charles Wesley earlier expressed the same thought. If you know anything about the Wesley brothers, John and Charles, you know that before they came to faith in Jesus Christ, they lived outwardly impeccable lives. Charles was a clergyman in the Church of England. No chains were visible. He had no apparent addictions. In his student days at the University of Oxford, he was marked by rigorous moral rectitude and energetic service. Few imagined they could match his holiness. One of his favorite books was titled *A Serious Call to a Devout and Holy Life*.[5] That summed him up.

Yet as God worked in Wesley's life, he realized he was in spiritual bondage, "fast bound in sin and nature's night,"[6] as he would later write. But when he was brought to faith in Jesus Christ, this was the song he wanted to sing again and again on the anniversary of his conversion:

My chains fell off, my heart was free,
I rose, went forth and followed thee.[7]

Such freedom is not limited to a select group of famous Christians. The gospel promises the same to everyone who trusts in Christ.

Freedom from bondage is a central theme in the teaching of our Lord Jesus Christ. He told the Jews of His day that only the gospel could release them: "The truth shall make you free" (John 8:32). But what truth? He explained: "If the Son makes you free, you shall be free indeed" (John 8:36).

Here are two basic lessons.

LESSON ONE—BONDAGE

Jesus taught that we are all by nature in spiritual bondage. He had to be cruel to be kind.

The Jews to whom Jesus spoke—much like us—believed that they were certainly not in bondage to anything. But their response to Jesus' words revealed the deep spiritual bondage in which they were held. His words riled and angered them.

"Who do you think you are, saying that we need to be set free? How dare you! We are Abraham's children, his freeborn descendents." They claimed spiritual freedom as their birthright, but they were in spiritual bondage.

"Most assuredly, I say to you," Jesus said, "whoever commits sins is a slave of sin" (John 8:34).

Does this really need to be underlined? Jesus thought it did, and perhaps someone reading these pages may need a little help to understand what Jesus was saying here:

- We do not become sinners by committing specific acts.
- We commit specific acts of sin because we are sinners.

In short, my problem is not the isolated actions that I see as *aberrations* from what I really am. I am deceiving myself if I think that way. These actions are not *aberrations* but *revelations* of what is in my heart. They show that I commit sin because I am in bondage to it.

Paul develops this theme in Ephesians 2. Both the apostle and his readers (v. 3) were by nature bound in sin: "dead in trespasses and sins" (v. 1). When they heard the name of God and of His grace in Jesus Christ, their hearts remained cold. Like dead men and women, they were always flowing with the stream, following "the course of this world" (v. 2).

By nature, we usually deny that we are in spiritual bondage. We go out of our way to show our freedom by being different. But we tend, in one way or another, to become clones. That is a manifestation of our bondage. According to Ray Davies' satirical lyrics in The Kinks' hit song,

This pleasure-seeking individual always looks his best
'Cause he's a dedicated follower of fashion.[8]

Of course, there is a darker side to this in the sinister influence of "the prince of the power of the air, the spirit who now works in the sons of disobedience" (v. 2). We will say much more about him later.

As Jesus hinted, this sinfulness affects every dimension of our lives:

• Our minds. We do not think clearly. We may be well educated and have high IQs. But that is no guarantee that we think clearly about spiritual things.

• Our desires. When we are on our own and at our most honest, we recognize that we are not masters of our desires. We try to master them. We have a moral consciousness that says, "You must get these things under control." But inwardly we are out of control. There is a world within us over which we have no mastery.

• Our wills. They are in bondage to sin. "Oh yes," we say, "this message about being right with God—I will come to it another day. That is my decision and I can make it whenever I want."

The truth, however, is that we cannot think clearly about or desire Christ by our own unaided decision. Why not? We cannot respond to the good news of the gospel until we want Christ, and we cannot want Christ simply by a decision we can take at any moment we choose. We cannot say to our will, "Will, will to belong to the Lord!" It is beyond our powers to do that. No one can will the will to will what it will not will! Only God's grace can set us free to come to trust in Him.

What made it happen so?
His own will, this much I know,
Set me, as now I show,
At liberty.

Here, then, is our greatest need. Lesson one: We are in bondage to sinful hearts.

David's Understanding of Sin

King David made this discovery months after his sin with Bathsheba. He had broken God's law. He had coveted, he had committed adultery, he had stolen the wife of one of the best men he knew, and he had plotted the man's death (see 2 Sam. 11–12).

When the reality of his spiritual bondage came home to David, he realized it went back to the very beginning of his life: "I was sinful . . . from the time my mother conceived me" (Ps. 51:5, NIV).

When we are first convicted of sin, we resolve to do better. But as soon as we have scraped away one layer of sin (thinking, "It was only a superficial failure on my part"), we discover another layer underneath. Until David traced his sin right back to the beginning of his life, he was living in a state of spiritual denial. But when he realized the truth about himself, he admitted that the rot had set in from the start, even when he was in his mother's womb. Then he cried out to God, "Cleanse me" (Ps. 51:7, NIV), or, "Scrub me clean."

There were times in my childhood when I got so dirty that my mother would scrub me clean with a loofah. How often I felt the power of her arm as she scrubbed the dirt out of my skin. While I was relatively content with a superficial wash, she was determined to get out all the dirt, even if it killed her—or *me*.

David's language—"cleanse me . . . wash me"—is an appeal for that kind of vigorous and rigorous cleansing. His sin was deep dyed. There were layers of deceptiveness, sin, and bondage in his heart. Only God could cleanse and free him.

This is what Jesus was talking about. His contemporaries knew their Bibles. They were in constant attendance at religious services. But they were still bound by sin and could not free their lives from its dominion. They were slaves to sin, not sons of God. So Jesus said to them, "Your fundamental problem is that you do not know God as your Father."

How could Jesus be so sure? "Because," He said, "if you really knew the Father, your attitude to His Son would be completely different. It would be one of love and of admiration. You would trust Me" (see John 8:42–47).

They talked about God, but their attitude to God's Son revealed that they were not members of His family. They were hostile to Him. They plotted "religiously" to get rid of Him. They had no place for Him in their lives because they had no room for His Father.

Deserving Nothing

Religious people are always profoundly disturbed when they discover that they are not, and never have been, true Christians. Does all of their religion count for nothing? Those hours in church, hours spent doing good things, hours involved in religious activity—do they not count for something in the presence of God? Do they not enable me to say: "Look at what I have done. Don't I deserve heaven?"

Sadly, thinking that I deserve heaven is a sure sign I have no understanding of the gospel.

Jesus unmasked the terrible truth about His contemporaries. They resisted His teaching and refused to receive His Word because they were sinners—and slaves to sin.

Some years ago, the British media reported that a Presbyterian denomination had pulled fifty thousand printed copies of an edition of its monthly magazine. The report indicated that the author of an article had referred to a prominent member of the British royal family as a "miserable sinner."

Intriguingly, the member of the royal family, as a member of the Church of England, must have regularly used the words of the Anglican prayer book's "Prayer of General Confession," which includes a request for the forgiveness of the sins of "miserable offenders." Why, then, were the magazines pulled? The official comment: "We don't want to give the impression that the doctrines of the Christian faith cause people emotional trauma."

But sometimes the doctrines of the Christian faith do exactly that—and necessarily so.

Or should we say instead: "How cruel Jesus was to these poor Jews! Fancy Jesus speaking to them in this way!"?

Jesus *did* say, "You are miserable sinners." He unmasked sinners and drove His point home: "You have no room for my word" (John 8:37, NIV). They had heard, but resisted it. Later, He described the result: "Why is my language not clear to you? Because you are unable to hear what I say" (John 8:43, NIV).

Jesus had already patiently explained this to Nicodemus: "Unless God's Spirit opens your eyes, you cannot see the kingdom of God. Unless God sets you free from the bondage of sin, you will never enter the kingdom of God" (see John 3:3, 5). "The truth is," Jesus said later, "you do not hear what I am saying because you are not really the children of God" (see John 8:41, 44). They were, to use Paul's language, spiritually "dead" (Eph. 2:1).

Some time ago, while relaxing on vacation on a wonderful summer day in the Scottish Highlands, I sat outside enjoying a morning coffee. A few feet away I saw a beautiful little red robin. I admired its feathers, its lovely red breast, its sharp and clean beak, its simple beauty. I found myself instinctively talking to it. But there was no response, no movement. Everything was intact, but little robin red-breast was dead. The most skilled veterinarian in the world could do absolutely nothing for him.

So are we, spiritually. Despite appearances, in my natural state I am dead toward God. There is no spiritual life in me.

Only when I see this will I begin to see why God's grace is surprising and amazing. For it is to spiritually dead people that the grace of God comes to give life and release.

This is the first truth I need to acknowledge. I am in spiritual bondage. That bondage may have many manifestations. They may differ from individual to individual. But the bondage itself is at root one and the same.

On that basis, and against that background, Jesus taught lesson number two.

LESSON TWO—FREEDOM

There is good news.

On the one hand, Jesus underlined the bondage in which we are held by nature. On the other hand, He spoke about the freedom into which He brings sinners by grace: "If the Son makes you free, you shall be free indeed" (John 8:36).

How could the Son set them free? Because of who He was. He was the Son who has been sent into the world by the Father. He knew the Father's plan. He had the most intimate relationship with the Father. He had heard everything the Father had said, and He came with this message of good news: "The Father has sent Me in order to set you free" (see John 8:28).

How, then, does Christ set us free?

John had answered that question earlier, in the most famous verse in his Gospel. This God, this Father, so loved the world, this world in its sinfulness and bondage, that He sent His only Son into it. He had only one Son, but He sent Him to die on a cross in order to save everyone who believes in Him (John 3:16).

The Son would be "lifted up"—lifted up on a cross, exposed in public shame, hanging between heaven and earth, under the judgment of God against our sins—so that those who believed in Him should not perish but have everlasting life (John 12:32; 3:16).

Jesus Christ is able to set us free because He has dealt with the sin that enslaves us.

We can never atone for our own sin. We can never break its power. We can never come to God and say, "God, surely what I have done is enough to compensate for my sins." Nothing we can do can possibly compensate. But God sent His own Son—think of it, *His own Son*—who stood in for us, in our place. He lived a perfect life. Since He had no sins of His own to atone for, He was qualified to make a sacrifice for our sins. No sacrifice we could make could ever be adequate to atone for sin. But He was able and willing to do it. Because of that, we can be set free from guilt and from the bondage it creates.

Christ also sets us free in another way: through the truth about God—and about ourselves—that He reveals. If we believe in Him, we will come to know the truth, and the truth will set us free (John 8:32). That is His promise.

I have met some exceptionally intelligent people who cannot understand the Christian gospel. They hear its message as if it were a lecture on morality. Yet the gospel is not difficult to understand. The problem lies within us—in our spiritual blindness. If there is resistance in the heart to *loving* God, there will be resistance in the mind to *knowing* God—and therefore to listening to and seeking God. Only the truth can set us free.

Later on in John's Gospel, Jesus spoke about sending the Holy Spirit to His disciples. He would be like a great spotlight shining into their minds, illumining them so that they could begin to see and understand Jesus and what He had done. The Spirit would remove spiritual deception, transform the spiritually dead, and glorify Christ.

So Jesus is able to set us free because of who He is and because of what He shows us.

As a result, we now may dare to call God "Father."

This is the most obvious difference between a "religious" person and a Christian. A religious person is likely to address God—especially in a crisis—as "O God," not as "O Father." There is a simple reason for this. Unless you know God as your Father, you never cry out to Him in your need as "Abba, Father" (Rom. 8:15–16).

Many Bondages, One Remedy

How does all of this apply to us?

Our sinful hearts share a common bondage, although its forms may differ. Some people have bondages that bring them down to the gutter. But there are also "respectable" bondages. The appearances may seem polar opposites. But in each the heart is equally captive, a prisoner, a slave.

What is it that you cannot master, but masters you? What sin has captured your heart and hardened it toward God? The chains that bind you may seem very different from those that bind your neighbors, your colleagues, or your friends. But they are just as real.

God has many different ways to bring us to discover that we are enslaved and spiritually dead sinners. But He offers us only one remedy for the slavery, only one Savior: the same Jesus who stood before His contemporaries—and now stands before us—to say:

"Whoever commits sin is the slave of sin. But the truth will set you free. And because I am the Son of God and the Savior, I can set you free.

"I am the One who has been working in your life recently.

"I am the One who has prompted you to ask questions you long ignored and to remember sins you once trivialized.

"I am the One who has led you to ask why a Christian you know has something you lack.

"All this has brought you to seek Me. You have now come to the verge of trusting in Me as the Savior who will set you free and give you a new life.

"You are beginning to see why grace is so wonderfully amazing.

"Trust Me now."

Charles Wesley wrote:

Long my imprisoned spirit lay,
Fast bound in sin and nature's night.[9]

Is that you? You may have tried everything to find freedom and satisfaction, but you are still "fast bound in sin and nature's night." Perhaps nobody knows it except you. You need a work of God's power and grace in your life.

Thine eye diffused a quickening ray,
I woke, the dungeon flamed with light.
My chains fell off, my heart was free
I rose, went forth, and followed thee.[10]

Discovering the grace of God in Jesus Christ can happen almost before you notice it. After all, He was seeking you before you ever sought Him or sensed that He was near. All you knew was that you had a deep sense of need. He drew you in, and you said to Him: "Be mine. Be my Savior!" He said to you: "I am. Be Mine, My child."

O how the grace of God
Amazes me!
It loosed me from my bonds
And set me free!

What made it happen so?
His own will, this much I know,
Set me, as now I show,
At liberty.

Freedom, at last!
Yes, grace is amazing.

2

―――

My God has chosen me,
Though one of nought,
To sit beside my King
In heaven's court.
Hear what my Lord has done
O, the love that made him run
To meet his erring son!
This has God wrought.

Chapter Two

UNCONDITIONAL LOVE

The grace of God is able to free us from our bondages. We may try to convince ourselves that they are nonexistent or even trivial. But when we try to free ourselves from them, we discover that we are just as powerless to do so as we have been helpless to resist them. Then we begin to see how much we need God's grace—and why it is so amazing.

No one ever discovers the nature of God's grace without first discovering the reason he or she needs it. The second verse of E. T. Sibomana's hymn "O How the Grace of God Amazes Me" underlines this:

My God has chosen me,
Though one of nought,
To sit beside my King
In heaven's court.
Hear what my Lord has done
O, the love that made him run
To meet his erring son!
This has God wrought.

You probably recognize the allusion in these last three lines. They echo the response of the father of the prodigal when he saw his son returning from the far country (Luke 15:11–32). The son had wasted his life and probably a third of the family fortune. But as he returned home, his father saw him (how long had he been waiting and watching for him?) and ran to meet him.

This parable of Jesus has been given a variety of titles. The best known, of course, is "The parable of the prodigal son." But as we shall see, there are actually three sons in this story.

Parables

Why did Jesus use parables in His teaching? Apparently not for the reason we often think.

People often say to Christian preachers: "Why don't you tell more stories—like Jesus did? We can understand stories. Jesus made things simple for us to understand."

But Jesus Himself placed a serious question mark beside that statement. In connection with His parables, He said: "For whoever has, to him more will be given, and he will have abundance; but whoever does not have, even what he has will be taken away from him. Therefore I speak to them in parables, because seeing they do not see, and hearing they do not hear, nor do they understand" (Matt. 13:12–13).

Jesus used parables so that those who thought they could see might be blinded, and those who were conscious they were blind might be able to see.

Understanding a parable is like solving the Rubik's Cube. If you know the key to doing it—as I remember my oldest son did—the multicolored cube can be perfectly restored to its original order in a matter of seconds, no matter how mixed up it has been. It can even be done with hands behind the back. It's a puzzle—if you don't know the secret. But if you have the key, everything fits into place.

It is exactly the same with parables. Without the key, the meaning and intent of Jesus' stories elude us. Miss the key and you miss the message.

What, then, is the secret? It is Jesus Christ Himself. The parables teach us how He establishes His kingdom in a totally unexpected way.

Lost Things

Luke 15 contains three parables. In some ways, they are three parts of one larger parable—a single message about lost things being found, each episode told in a context of increased complexity and heightened tension.

Scene one describes a shepherd who has lost one of his sheep. Sheep were, and are, valuable. But he has lost only one out of a hundred—one percent.

Scene two describes a woman who has lost a silver coin. The coin is valuable to her; perhaps it was saved for a rainy day. She has lost one coin out of ten—ten percent, a much higher percentage loss.

The third scene, however, is much more poignant. The father of two sons loses one of them. He has lost fifty percent of his sons, not a sheep or a coin—an unbearable loss.

Jesus was clearly building up to the main point. The scenes in the third parable are described at much greater length, with much greater complexity and intensity of emotion. In addition, there are more characters in the third story—two sons and their father—each of whom expresses his thoughts and feelings about the situation.

Furthermore, each of them clearly reflects the context in which Jesus was speaking.

Tax collectors and "sinners" were gathering around to listen—He drew them like a magnet. Perhaps some of them had seen their friends dramatically transformed by Him.

When the Pharisees and the teachers of the law saw what was happening, they muttered, "This Man receives sinners and eats with them" (Luke 15:2).

The Pharisees were a Jewish "sect" committed to the detailed observance of the law. They had added stringent extra-biblical rules as to the exact ways in which people should keep the law.

The "teachers of the law" were experts in the interpretation of these traditions.

A Life Devoted to Law

As I write these words, I am sitting on an airplane bound for Tel Aviv. Many Jews are on board. The clothing worn by some of them indicates that they are Hasidic Jews, in some respects the heirs of the Pharisees and teachers of the law.

Earlier, in the terminal, the men gathered for prayers, and they have done so again during the flight. One of them should have been seated between me and the lady who is seated in the window seat in my row. I watched the discomfort on his face as he checked his boarding pass. He found another seat rather than sit beside the woman—herself, as I have discovered, Jewish. (He knows nothing of the wonderful way in which Christ has brought Jewish and Gentile believers into one body.)

I have been watching this particular man during the overnight flight. He has spent most of it poring over his commentary on Torah. He desires to be like the righteous man of Psalm 1, who meditates on God's law day and night. He belongs to a people apart. Studying Torah through the traditions of the rabbis is his life. But he does not know that while Torah came by Moses, grace and truth came through Jesus Christ (John 1:17).

So it was with the Pharisees and teachers of the law. They were a separated people. The great temptation for such people is to feel not only separated but better. After all, they are "the faithful," others are "sinners." Then they begin to suspect good men who mingle with those who are not faithful, even if untouched by their moral failures. In order to be holy, one must not mingle with those who are unholy.

Jesus befriended tax collectors and sinners. So the Pharisees and scribes muttered criticisms of Him behind His back.

Here, then, we find a trio of figures: (1) tax collectors and sinners, (2) Pharisees and teachers of the law, and (3) Jesus Himself. When we turn to the second half of the chapter, to the story of the man who had two sons, we find that there are also three characters in the story. We should not lose sight of that connection.

There is the father—he "stands for" Jesus, who had been fiercely accused and condemned: "This Man receives sinners and eats with them" (Luke 15:2).

Then there are two sons (Luke 15:11), a younger and an older brother.

Like many truly great stories—certainly the great Bible stories—this one invites us to read it through the eyes of each of the characters involved in the drama. It is a story with more than one perspective. If we are going to see the whole picture, we need to focus not only on the younger son (the "prodigal"), but also to look through the eyes of both the father and the elder brother.

THE VIEW FROM THE FAR COUNTRY—THE PRODIGAL

Here is a young man. He is single. He wants to throw off all the restraints of family life. He demands from his father, as his right, his share in the family property and wealth. He should—of course—have waited.

Like all the parables in the Bible, this one is full of little signals that must have touched the hearts and minds of its first hearers.

The younger son says to his father, "Give me the share of property that is coming to me" (v. 12, ESV). So the father divides his property between his two sons. Literally, the father is said to divide his "life" (bios, v. 12b).

This story is about life—and death. Later on, the language of "dead" and "alive" will be used. This young man wants life, but he looks for it in the wrong place. What he finds is a living death. Then, marvelously, he is brought from death to life (v. 24).

The Offense and the Shame

Jesus' first hearers must have felt the deep offensiveness of this son's request. It is multidimensional:

• He is the younger son. More than anything else, he wants to be free from the "restrictiveness" of life in the family home, where the father's plans and pleasures are foremost. He wants to "enjoy life" without restraints. He insults his father.

• "*Give* me," he says to his father. "Give me my share of life. Give me my own way in life." Clearly the subtext of what he is saying is, "I don't want to wait until you die to get my share of the inheritance." In other words (not to put too fine a point on it): "As far as I am concerned, you can drop dead today. I don't care. I just want my own life." He despises his father.

• The father is a substantial landowner. But land must be sold before it can realize its monetary value. Faced with the need to sell land quickly to meet his son's demand, this father stands to take a big loss when other local landowners see a prime opportunity to increase their own wealth at a discount price. More than that, if this man sells a major portion of his land, that land is likely gone forever. If he gives away such a major portion of his estate, the prospect of redeeming it is small. The son impoverishes his father.

The hearers, drawn into the story, knew that the younger son's demand was not only offensive, it was destructive. Such a son could only destroy himself—and perhaps eventually destroy his father also. Such a son should be rejected forever. Indeed, a rebellious son like this was viewed as forfeiting his right to life.

How could a successful father, with every reason to be content with his achievements, ever raise his head in public again after this rejection by his younger son?

Echoes of the Past

The rest of the story is a brilliant telling of the expected. The young man who grasps for life ends up in a "far country." He is dead as far as the family is concerned.

In storytelling traditions, narratives are full of verbal clues that serve as signposts to alert listeners. For example, in children's stories, the appearance of a stepmother usually prepares us for the cruelty and danger the stepchild (usually the heroine) will experience before some great act of deliverance takes place.

The first hearers of Jesus' parable were much more skilled listeners than we tend to be. As people who delighted in the telling and hearing of stories, they looked for, recognized, and enjoyed the verbal signs and echoes that evoked emotions associated with other stories with which they were familiar.

Jesus' story contained clues like this. Those who listened might well have been reminded of other biblical stories where individuals snatched at life, foolishly wishing themselves free from restraint. They might have thought of Jacob, the twister, who also ended up in a "far country," or of the first man, Adam, whose life ended outside Eden.

God surrounded Adam with the rich blessings of life. But he wanted life on his own terms and in his own way—free from the "restraints" placed on him by the Father. So he stretched out his hand to take the forbidden fruit, the temptation heavily leveraged by the fact that the woman he loved had already done so.

Alas, Adam and Eve discovered that by snatching for what they wanted apart from God, they lost both God *and* what they wanted. Instead of experiencing life, they tasted death. They ended up in a "far country"—an expression that also surely reminded Jesus' hearers of the exile in Babylon and banishment from the presence of God.

That is where this young man is heading. He is not simply emigrating; he is making a disastrous pilgrimage away from security and plenty. The father's house is a "land flowing with milk and honey" (Ex. 3:8). But he wants something different. There in the far country, exiled from his father, he squanders his inheritance on what the New International Version vividly calls "wild living." He wastes everything (v. 13). Tragically, he ends up wishing he could have the same diet as the pigs for which he (a Jew) is responsible (v. 16).

What a tragic fall. He has flashed across the sky like a brilliant meteor; now he is a spent force. He wanted everything; now he has nothing.

> *But pleasures are like poppies spread,*
> *You seize the flow'r, its bloom is shed.*[11]

Coming to Ourselves

Then, amazingly, comes the turning point. The prodigal "came to himself" or "came to his senses" (v. 17, NIV). What did Jesus mean?

The younger brother begins to see himself and his situation in a new light. He remembers his father. How far away he has drifted. How far down he has fallen. How arrogant he has been. How self-absorbed. Now he is spent. He threw himself confidently into finding satisfaction, but he has become the epitome of the dissatisfied man. Long before the Rolling Stones, he could have sung:

I can't get no satisfaction.
I can't get no satisfaction.
'Cause I try and I try and I try and I try.
I can't get no, I can't get no. . . .[12]

This is the story of every man or woman who turns his or her back on God. We seek to silence the warning voice of conscience. But we can never wholly succeed. Not all the iPods in the world can drown out the memory of home. Unable to pacify it, we must harden our hearts against the God who warns us through it.

Of course, we mask that hostility. But we can never fully hide it.

Sometimes it is clearer to others than it is to us that we are running from God. Our negative, embarrassed, or hostile reactions to Christians, to the name of Jesus, to references to the greatness, wonder, and goodness of God and His works—all are telltale signs. We are far from intellectually or personally objective about, or indifferent to, God. Underneath it all, we are opposed to Him emotionally and intellectually; otherwise, why so much resentment?

This is the situation of the prodigal. He has a warped view of his father and now carefully defends himself against the truth. He thought he could permanently sustain that defense. But nobody can sustain it forever.

It is simply not possible to build up a consistent self-defense against the inroads and incursions of God. There is not a square yard in the universe to which an individual can go where he can say, "I can hide here from God and escape from Him." God is already there. He has made Himself known in the whole of creation. Nowhere is a "safe house."

This is the point Paul makes so powerfully in Romans 1:

For the wrath of God is revealed from heaven against all ungodliness and unrighteousness of men, who suppress the truth in unrighteousness, because what may be known of God is manifest in them, for God has shown it to them. For since the creation of the world His invisible attributes are clearly seen, being understood by the things that are made, even His eternal power and Godhead, so that they are without excuse, because although they knew God, they did not glorify Him as God, nor were thankful, but became futile in their thoughts, and their foolish hearts were darkened. Professing to be wise, they became fools, and changed the glory of the incorruptible God into an image made like corruptible man—and birds and four-footed animals and creeping things. (Rom. 1:18–23)

The prodigal felt that, at last, he was away from his father. He could forget about home. The past would never return to haunt him. His father could never find him, even if he tried. But he finds he cannot escape so easily, even in a far country. Not even a pigpen is a place of escape. He cannot shut out from his mind, his memory, and his conscience the knowledge that is built into his very being: he is a sinful, rebellious, wayward child of a caring father. He cannot pull down the shutters and blot out the memory of home.

No more can we be secure against the heavenly Father.

Coming Home

What does the erring son do? He says to himself, "I will arise and go to my father, and will say to him, 'Father, I have sinned against heaven and before you'" (v. 18). That is good. He realizes his life is a disaster. He now knows himself to be, as Pastor Sibomana's hymn puts it, "one of nought."

He rehearses his homecoming speech: "I have sinned against heaven and before you, and I am no longer worthy to be called your son. Make me like one of your hired servants" (vv. 18–19).

Jesus' hearers knew what a prodigal could expect if he returned home: the *kezazah* ceremony, in which the father's wrath would be publicly vented against his son.[13]

"Treat me as a servant," the son plans to say. This is an expression of the natural instinct of men and women whose hearts have been awakened to their sin and need. Their first instinct is to say: "I will pull myself together. I will begin to do things that will please God. From now on, I will do better at keeping his law. I will change my lifestyle. I will try harder. I will work my way back into his favor."

So the prodigal begins to make his long way back home with this thought in his mind: "Perhaps as I do better, I can make my life over again. Although I can never become a son again, perhaps I can repay some of the debt I owe to my father and try to balance my rebellion with obedience. Perhaps I can make up if I am prepared to confess I was wrong."

So he returns to his father.

Now comes the shock.

Jesus continues: "But when he was still a great way off, his father saw him and had compassion, and ran and fell on his neck and kissed him. And the son said to him, 'Father, I have sinned against heaven and in your sight, and am no longer worthy to be called your son . . .'" (vv. 20–21).

Is the family home on a hillside? What instinct makes the father look into the distance ("he was still a great way off")? How does the father recognize him? Is he in the habit of looking into the distance, wishing, wondering, praying? Has he never lost hope? Some of the silences in Jesus' storytelling are stimulating and evocative; that is part of His genius as a storyteller.

Then the moment of moments comes. The father *runs* from his vantage point—either down the hill or along the village street.

So long as we think, "Of course he ran—his son was coming home," we will never be able to hear this parable the way Jesus' contemporaries did. "An Oriental nobleman with flowing robes never runs anywhere."[14]

Furthermore, given the dishonor the son has done to his father by leaving home, this man's actions must amaze his watching neighbors. This is an astonishing sight. Indeed, it is almost certainly scandalous.

As the father reaches his son, the oft-rehearsed words are forming on the prodigal's lips. But already his father is embracing him, kissing him. Tears are beginning to flow.

The words begin to pour out from his heaving body: "Father . . . , I have sinned against heaven . . . and you. I am . . . no longer . . . worthy to be called your son. . . . Make me . . ." But the well-rehearsed words, *"like one of your hired servants,"* are never heard. They are interrupted by this loving, welcoming, forgiving—yes, fussing—father.

Luke writes: "But the father said to his servants, 'Bring out the best robe and put it on him, and put a ring on his hand and sandals on his feet. And bring the fatted calf here and kill it, and let us eat and be merry; for this my son was dead and is alive again; he was lost and is found.' And they began to be merry" (vv. 22–24).

We do not need to have detailed knowledge of the ancient Near East to get the message: from death to life; from lost to found; from poverty in the pigpen to the robe, ring, shoes, fattened calf, and celebratory party. This is the universal language of joy. Amazingly, the father does not punish his wayward son, but forgives him, restores him, enriches him, and blesses him.

The father's embrace of forgiveness means that his returning son never says the last sentence of his carefully crafted speech. This father will not have his son home as a hired hand or a household servant. This is his son. The father welcomes him home not to be a slave but a son raised from the dead and adopted back into the family.

Yes, all this about sinning against heaven and in his father's sight is true, tragically so. But the father has dealt with that. He has taken the shame and humiliation himself. He bears all the cost of the forgiveness and restoration of his "wayward son."

Has the father changed? Has pain mellowed him?

No, he has always been this generous father. But he has a son who, through the deep pain of repentance, has learned the difference between "give me" (v. 12) and "make me" or "treat me" (v. 19, ESV).

Amazing grace!—how sweet the sound—
That saved a wretch like me!
I once was lost, but now am found,
Was blind, but now I see.[15]

THE VIEW FROM THE FIELDS—THE ELDER BROTHER

So much for the story as seen through the eyes of the prodigal who discovers grace. But there is another perspective, because there is an elder brother in the parable.

This second brother is not incidental to the story. In many ways, he is as central as his more famous younger brother.

The parables of Jesus illustrate an important principle of all good story-telling. Scholars sometimes refer to it as "the principle of end stress."

We use a similar principle when we tell jokes or amusing stories. The "punch line" is never in the middle; it is always at the end. If the punch line comes too soon, the joke falls flat and nobody laughs. It is excruciating for both teller and hearer alike. The punch line is called "the punch line" precisely because it takes people by surprise—like a punch—and (unlike a punch) its unexpectedness produces laughter.

The same is true of Jesus' parables. We usually need to read right to the end to get the punch line. In this parable, it takes us by surprise. The "punch line" depends on the presence of the elder brother.

Pharisees Unmasked

At the beginning of Luke 15, we are told that Jesus "spoke this parable to *them*" (v. 3, emphasis added). Who? "The Pharisees and scribes [who] complained" (v. 2). Jesus was pointing the finger in this parable at those who criticized Him for welcoming sinners and eating with them.

The elder brother was Jesus' portrayal—indeed, His unmasking—of these Jewish leaders. He had poured out grace on sinful men and women, and they had responded to His message about the kingdom of God. They came to Him to receive love, forgiveness, welcome, and restoration. But the Pharisees were repelled by the grace the Lord Jesus displayed and utterly demeaned Him for it—as well as despising those who received it.

Jesus vividly portrayed the spirit of these men in the elder brother. When he hears the sound of celebration, he comes in from the fields, grits his teeth, and demands to know what is happening. He learns the news, but he refuses to go in or share any part of the celebration.

Grace, you would think, would make him happy. But it makes the elder brother miserable. He seems incapable of either receiving or rejoicing in grace.

What irritates the older brother about grace is precisely that it is grace. In his eyes, the younger son does not deserve what he is receiving. Has his father no sense of justice? The tragedy is that he himself has never enjoyed a relationship of grace with his father.

What a picture of a person whose religion has no place for grace, and who therefore never experiences it. His religion is his bondage, not his freedom. He is held captive by what Paul calls a "spirit of bondage" (Rom. 8:15). He is a tragic figure indeed.

The elder brother lives within the family compound and has every possible opportunity to be close to his father. But there is a distance between him and the father that—even at the end of the parable—remains unbridged.

The Pharisees and scribes were pictured in the elder brother. They knew Torah—probably by heart. Of them, Jesus would say, "You search the Scriptures, for in them you think you have eternal life" (John 5:39). But then He added, sadly, "But you are not willing to come to Me that you may have life" (v. 40). The story of the elder brother is itself a parable on John 5:39–40, set within the larger parable of Luke 15.

The Tragedy

Religion can be bad for your spiritual health. Engaging in religious duties (even good ones) can be very deceptive. It can dis-grace grace. The Pharisees saw no need to come to Christ—after all, they were searching the Scriptures.

Jesus put His finger on another characteristic of graceless religion. There is no indication in the parable that the family received news about the prodigal son from the far country. The father seems to assume that he is dead. But when the prodigal comes home, the elder brother engages in a diatribe against him. Its chief characteristic is that it focuses on what grace would have covered over ("love will cover a multitude of sins," 1 Peter 4:8): "As soon as this son of yours came, who has devoured your livelihood with harlots, you killed the fatted calf for him" (Luke 15:30). Notice the hurtful distance the son creates from his father: *"this son of yours"*—not "my brother." Now the elder brother sees himself as superior not only to his brother but also to his father. He rubs his brother's sins in his father's face.

This is often a characteristic of many religious people, who do not taste the grace of God and who have never experienced or enjoyed the forgiveness of sins. Why should they desire what they think they do not need? After all, their track record is surely acceptable to God, is it not? They are better than most. They are not perfect, of course, but what can be expected? Grace, if needed, is due them. They stress the faults of others to emphasize the point. They speak the language of the elder brother: "As soon as *this son of yours* . . ."

Notice what graciousness the father shows the elder brother: "All that I have is yours" (v. 31). But his elder son will have none of it.

Here, then, are two sure signs that our religion, even if we call it Christian, is not the real thing. We are not made happy by seeing the grace of God touch the lives of needy men and women so that they are brought to faith in Jesus Christ, and we neither see nor feel any special need for forgiveness for ourselves. We do not see ourselves as "one of nought."

There is a third sign. "Lo, these many years I have been serving you; I never transgressed your commandment at any time; and yet you never gave me a young goat that I might make merry with my friends" (v. 29). The New International Version translation is more vivid and expressive: "All these years I've been *slaving* for you . . ." (emphasis added).

Is this your religion—not the freedom of a son but the bondage of a slave? Is the Christian life a burden for you? Does it irritate you to see others "getting something for nothing" while you feel so little real joy in the Lord? That is the elder brother. Is it you also?

The elder brother holds the title to great riches. Yet he speaks like a complaining child: "You never give me anything. You never let me do anything." This is our Lord's picture of the spirit of bondage, not the Spirit of sonship (Rom. 8:15).

THE VIEW FROM THE HOME—THE FATHER

Thankfully, there is a third perspective in this parable: that of the father.

The father in this parable is often thought of as a picture of the heavenly Father. But in the context, Jesus was picturing Himself. He is the shepherd who rescues the lost sheep. He is the woman who finds the lost coin. He is the father who welcomes the prodigal son.

What, then, does this tell us about Jesus? There is something scandalous about the freedom of the father's grace. He runs to meet his son and lavishes on him forgiveness and assurance. He throws his arms around the prodigal and kisses him. He bestows on him marks of his love. "Bring out the best robe." Has he been keeping it in hope against hope that his son might return? "Put a ring on his hand." In the ancient Near East, this was a mark of authority, sometimes even royalty. "Put sandals on his feet." Slaves did not wear sandals, nor did guests. Only family members wore sandals.

These are all indications that the father has no intention of receiving his lost son as a hired hand or of making him a permanent servant. He will have him in the family because he forgives him—because he loves him. He welcomes him not to servitude but to sonship. "Kill the fatted calf," he shouts with joy. "Let's have a feast and celebrate. For this son of mine who demanded life and found only death is alive again; he was in the pigpen in the far country, but now he is home!"

The Grace Party

Until you have come to the end of the journey home to faith in Jesus Christ, it is likely that all you expect deep down from Christ is punishment. But when the prodigal makes the journey, he discovers a family party.

The Gospels contain a number of references to celebrations and parties. This is wonderfully expressive of Jesus' view of what it means to belong to the kingdom of God, to the fellowship of His people, and to the church that He was beginning to build. We are invited to a celebration. Yes, there is another side to the Christian life, and it is expressed here—deep sorrow for sin, repentance, and costly grace. But joy in forgiveness is always there.

The Christian life may appear from the outside to be a very sober way. It is, in many respects. But from the inside, it is also a life of great joy. As you enter the kingdom of God, you encounter people who share in God's forgiveness and pardon.

You may have lived a life of moral abandonment and been far from Christ, and then been wonderfully brought to trust Him as Savior and Lord. Or you may have lived a life of severe religious discipline and, without realizing it, have drifted far from Christ. In either case, when you come to say, "Father, I have sinned against heaven and in your sight, and am no longer worthy to be called your son," before another word is out of your mouth, He embraces you. Then you realize that He has done more than pardon you and count you righteous. He has brought you into His family and made you His child.

Well, where are you? Home? Very close to home but never having really trusted the Savior? Or very far away from home and beginning to hear the Savior's voice?

What are you to do?

This parable is sometimes called "the parable of the two sons." But earlier we hinted that there are actually three sons.

THE THIRD SON

Have you recognized the *third* son?

Count the sons.

One left home and returned.

A second stayed at home but remained far away.

Where is the third son?

The third son is the Son who is telling the story. He is the Son who was at home with His Father but came to the far country. If we miss Him, we miss the meaning of the parable. For the characters in it—however true to life they may be—are imaginary. Jesus, however, is not. He is the One who, through costly grace and great humiliation, provides the way for prodigal sons to be welcomed home.

This is what the story is really all about. As He told it, Jesus was talking both to prodigal sons and elder brothers, and inviting them to come to Him, to trust in Him, and to experience the joy of being His.

Pastor Sibomana's hymn might well have been sung by the prodigal son.

My God has chosen me,
Though one of nought,
To sit beside my King

In heaven's court.
Hear what my Lord has done
O, the love that made him run
To meet his erring son!
This has God wrought.

Would that the elder brother might have sung along with him!

It is natural enough—and right—to ask: Where am I in this story? Do you see yourself? Are you the prodigal or the elder brother?

But it is even more important to ask: Do you see Jesus as your Savior in this story?

That is the place to begin.

3

Not for my righteousness,
For I have none,
But for his mercy's sake,
Jesus, God's Son,
Suffered on Calvary's tree—
Crucified with thieves was he—
Great was his grace to me,
His wayward one.

Chapter Three

AT GOD'S EXPENSE

"How the Grace of God Amazes Me" takes us, step by step, through various dimensions of God's saving grace. The third verse brings us to the theme of this chapter—salvation was costly to God. E. T. Sibomana writes:

Jesus, God's Son,
Suffered on Calvary's tree—
Crucified with thieves was he—
Great was his grace to me,
His wayward one.

A number of years ago, I heard former British Cabinet Minister Jonathan Aitken speak in private and in public about the loneliness he experienced when he was arrested for perjury, tried, found guilty, imprisoned, and—perhaps worst of all—publicly stripped of his reputation as a leading politician and a potential prime minister of Great Britain.

In God's grace, Aitken became a Christian.[16] He would now be the first to say that his loneliness, suffering, and loss of reputation, no matter how intensely he felt it, were minor by comparison with the depth of the loneliness and the intensity of the suffering of Jesus when He was arrested, tried, and condemned—in His case, unjustly.

The Gospel writers (perhaps especially Luke, who seems to have been unusually sensitive to these things) bring out the cost of salvation in the way they trace the last twenty-four hours of Jesus' life. The meaning of His passion is woven into the warp and woof of the narrative. These hours take us from the Passover meal He shared with His disciples in the upper room until the moment on Golgotha when He serenely bowed His head and committed His spirit into the hands of His heavenly Father.

Into Loneliness

The whole story of Jesus' passion, His arrest, His trial, His suffering, and His public execution is one of appalling loneliness and isolation voluntarily experienced in order to restore us to fellowship with God.

After the meal in the upper room, Jesus went to the Garden of Gethsemane. There He sought consolation from His Father and encouragement from His disciples. He took Peter, James, and John (His "inner circle") and separated them from the others in the group. Then He isolated Himself even from them, and was entirely on His own.

In the hours that followed, this movement into isolation continued and intensified. He was further separated from His disciples, friends, and family members—although they came, bravely, to be with Him at His execution. This was surely the hour the aged Simeon foresaw when he said to the young Mary, "a sword will pierce through your own soul" (Luke 2:35).

From His arrest until He was helped to carry His cross by Simon of Cyrene, Jesus had no close contact with human help—indeed, His one sighting of Simon Peter was when curses rang out from the disciple's lips (Matt. 26:74; Luke 22:61). Did Jesus also feel a sword piercing His soul as He heard the words, "I do not know the Man!"? Only at Golgotha did He have further contact with those who had known Him best and loved Him most.

But there was much more—and much worse. Jesus felt Himself to be abandoned by God and cried out on the cross: "My God, My God, why have You forsaken Me?" (Matt. 27:46).

As Luke tells the story, Jesus' trial took place in two parts: one religious, the other civil or secular. The religious leaders mocked him, as did the Roman soldiers. The (supposedly) heavenly minded conspired with the earthly minded to bring about the execution and destruction of Jesus of Nazareth.

Luke highlights his plot line by a series of questions about Jesus that are asked and answered as events unfold. They punctuate the whole passion narrative (Luke 22:47–23:56). In different ways, answers are given to the question, "What is really happening here in this flagrant miscarriage of justice?"

Luke crafts his narrative carefully. He selects scenes and words in order to help us to see the real issues. He shows us that there is a meaning to this apparently meaningless series of events. That meaning shines forth as the narrative begins to focus on questions about Jesus' identity.

SON OF MAN AND SON OF GOD?

The first of these questions was asked by the chief priests and the teachers of the law as they met in the Jewish ruling council (the Sanhedrin): "Are You then the Son of God?" (Luke 22:70).

They were not interested in the truth. They were engaged in what was essentially a form of torture, both mental and physical. Either they would destroy Jesus or He would destroy Himself by a confession of blasphemy.

The question, "Do you claim to be the Son of God?" arose because of what He had said: "Hereafter the Son of Man will sit on the right hand of the power of God" (v. 69).

The self-description "Son of Man" is used virtually exclusively by Jesus Himself. Outside of the Gospels, Stephen the martyr is the only other person who uses it: "I see the heavens opened and the Son of Man standing at the right hand of God!" (Acts 8:56).

Jesus' closest disciples—who heard Him use this title often—never seem to have referred to Him as "the Son of Man." But He is recorded as using it on about forty *different* occasions.

What are we meant to learn from this? Our Lord employed this favorite self-designation "Son of Man" in essentially three ways or contexts:

• When He described the humility of His life and service.

• When He spoke about the awfulness of the passion and the suffering He would experience.

• When He talked about His future enthronement and the splendor of the majesty and glory He anticipated would follow His death.

These three contexts suggest that "Son of Man" is not a reference to Jesus' human nature while "Son of God" expresses His divine nature. Certainly, the title "Son of Man" is used in the context of the lowliness of Jesus, to express humility and His humanity. But it involves much more than that.

The Vision of Daniel

Jesus' use of the title was derived in part from Daniel 7:13–14:

> I was watching in the night visions, and behold, One like the Son of Man, coming with the clouds of heaven! He came to the Ancient of Days, and they brought Him near before Him. Then to Him was given dominion and glory and a kingdom, that all peoples, nations, and languages should serve Him. His dominion is an everlasting dominion, which shall not pass away, and His kingdom the one which shall not be destroyed.

Daniel sees God the Father, the Ancient of Days, sitting enthroned in blazing majesty and glory, surrounded by His heavenly court. In his vision, someone comes on the clouds of heaven toward the Glorious One. He seems to be using the clouds as His triumphal chariot as He approaches the throne of the Majesty on High. He comes to the throne in order to be exalted. He receives from the Most High all authority in heaven and on earth.

This, of course, is a picture of the hidden identity of the Lord Jesus. He is this Son of Man. He is the only one who is qualified to sit down at the right hand of the Majesty on High.

Thus, by His use of "Son of Man," Jesus wove together the fact that He had come to share our human nature and to do for us what we have failed to do for ourselves. He came to minister to us and to suffer for us. But then

He went to take His rightful place again at the right hand of the Majesty on High as King of kings and Lord of lords. The Son of Man went from His humiliation to share the throne of exaltation, and He will share His triumph and glory with all of His saints (Dan. 7:18).

The religious leaders knew Daniel 7 well enough. When they asked, "Are You the Son of God?" and received Jesus' reply that they would see the Son of Man sitting at the right hand of the throne of God, they recognized His claim. They were abusing Him. He was their prisoner, humiliated, weak, destined for further rejection and shame. They were seeking to intimidate Him into a forced confession so that they might condemn Him without trial. But Jesus spoke to them with regal dignity: "The Son of Man will sit on the right hand of the power of God." They lunged in for the kill immediately, their knives sharpened to destroy him: "Are You then the Son of God?" He responded: "You rightly say that I am" (Luke 22:70). They replied: "We have heard it ourselves [i.e. blasphemy] from His own mouth" (v. 71).

Jesus certainly confessed His true identity. Yes.

But was He guilty of blasphemy? No.

These leaders did not investigate either the truthfulness or the legality of Jesus' claim. They had no interest in that. The claim itself was enough for them to cry: "Blasphemy! We do not need any more testimony. We need no longer try to bribe witnesses. We can dispense with due process. We have heard it from His own lips. We are witnesses that this man has claimed to be the Son of Man and the Son of God."

So they charged Jesus with, and condemned him for, blasphemy.

Changing the Charge

The appropriate punishment was death. But they knew—wily serpents that they were—that the charge would not be upheld by the secular authorities. It did not provide sufficient leverage to induce the Romans to have the Lord Jesus executed. After all, the theology of the Roman Empire left room for a whole pantheon of divine figures—what harm would another do, so long as it was also confessed that "Caesar is lord"?

As the narrative unfolds, the whole assembly arose and led Jesus off to Pontius Pilate.

But then the charges against Him changed. Before Pilate, they accused Him not of blasphemy but of subverting the nation, opposing payment of taxes to Caesar, and claiming to be "Christ, a King" (Luke 23:2).

Pontius Pilate, the Roman governor, was a greedy, cruel, inflexible man who despised the Jews and treated them with contempt. But by this stage in his life, his career seems to have been in jeopardy. That may well explain his weakness during the trial of Jesus. The very mention of the word *king* was enough to make him nervous.

This leads us into the second question that dominates this passage.

THE KING OF THE JEWS?

Question two formed on the lips of the Roman provincial governor. He asked an appropriate question, given the way Jesus had been brought before him. "What is the evidence for this charge of sedition?" Then, to Jesus: "Are You the King of the Jews?" (Luke 23:3a).

Jesus answered Pilate in terms similar to those with which He had answered the Sanhedrin: "It is as you say" (v. 3b).

Pilate may have been a cruel and bigoted Roman, but he was not naïve. Presumably overseas postings in the Roman foreign service involved some form of training program. Pilate had some inkling that the Jewish Scriptures promised that a messianic King would come. Indeed, in the very first scroll of their sacred books, there was an ominous promise of a coming Conqueror. Pilate knew well that their God—"*The Name*," as they called Him—had promised that He would establish a King of His own on the throne of David. The governor probably despised these prophecies, but he could not have been ignorant of them. Indeed, dealing with messianic hopes—which meant quelling them—was one of his most basic tasks as governor.

The Jewish leaders also knew what they were doing when they brought this humiliated figure to Pilate. The governor would be indifferent to the charge of blasphemy but extremely sensitive to that of treason. Therein lay their leverage. They knew he did not handle such situations well—and on this occasion, at least, they were sure they could use that to their advantage.

Their charge, therefore, was that Jesus was a threat to the *Pax Romana*. Any claim to kingship meant trouble for Rome. And trouble for Rome meant trouble for Pontius Pilate. This he had to avoid at all costs. He was only too familiar with messianic politics and their dangers. He knew all about guerilla warfare. He was constantly on the watch for intelligence on the various underground resistance organizations.

But now there stood before him—shamed, humiliated, abused, demeaned, sported with, intimidated, and deprived of sleep—Jesus of Nazareth.

Little could Pilate have realized that the next few hours would make him one of the most famous figures in all history, the only Roman political figure whose name is on the lips of millions of people on a weekly basis as they recite the Apostles' Creed in a hundred languages: "I believe . . . in Jesus Christ . . . who . . . *suffered under Pontius Pilate*. . . ."

Here, then, was the Man the priests and Sanhedrin claimed to be profoundly subversive. They had accused Him of blasphemy—to them the most heinous of all sins. Now they had added the accusation of treason, the subversion of Rome—the most serious of civil crimes.

What would Pilate do?

Charges: True or False?

All four Gospels make it clear that Pilate knew these charges were false. He tried—unsuccessfully—to extricate himself from the situation when he learned Jesus was from Galilee. That was Herod's jurisdiction. He knew that Herod was in town for the Passover and sent Jesus to him. But Herod and his soldiers simply abused Jesus and sent Him back to Pilate dressed in "a gorgeous robe" (Luke 23:11). Was that a signal to Pilate that, as far as Herod was concerned, he could do as he pleased? Was Herod saying he would stand with Pilate, no matter what?

Pilate still felt a sense of unease. Could this man really be guilty of treason? Could He really be an agent provocateur against Rome? Everything about

Him, despite the humiliation to which He obviously had been subjected, seemed dignified, gracious, poised, impressive.

Rather than accuse Jesus, Pilate found himself drawn into a discussion with Him. Something was profoundly wrong here—as his wife would later remind him ("Have nothing to do with that just man" she said, "for I have suffered many things today in a dream because of Him"; Matt. 26:19). There was no arrogant Jewish hostility here; this was no fanatic. Treason, treachery against the emperor? "No king but Caesar!" Pilate would hear the crowd cry. But there was a royal grace about this man. He spoke as though He were not subject to the might and power of Rome—indeed, not subject to any earthly power.

Thus, the unhappy Pontius Pilate was forced to investigate the capital charge. He would soon publicly (and with overdone theatrics) "wash his hands" of Jesus of Nazareth—or so he thought (little did he realize that the only thing for which he would be remembered in history would be his blood-stained hands). So the capital charge inexorably led to capital punishment.

This took place despite two facts.

First, Jesus patiently explained to Pilate that His reign was not a worldly political reign (John 18:33–38).

But even more significant is a second feature in Luke's account. He weaves into it a series of statements in which Jesus is declared to be innocent. Time and again as the charges are presented, Jesus is acknowledged to be, without reservation, not guilty of any and all of them.

This litany of acquittals is so impressive, it is worth pausing to notice in detail:

• Luke 23:4 (NIV): Pilate—"I find no basis for a charge against this man."

• Luke 23:14: Pilate—"Having examined Him in your presence, I have found no fault in this Man concerning those things of which you accuse Him."

• Luke 23:15: Pilate—"Nothing deserving of death has been done by Him."

• Luke 23:22: Pilate—"I have found no reason for death in Him."

• Luke 23:41 (NIV): One of the criminals crucified with Jesus—"We are punished justly, for we are getting what our deeds deserve. But this man has done nothing wrong."

• Luke 23:47: The Roman centurion in charge of the execution—"Certainly this was a righteous Man!"

Jesus was not falsely judged "Guilty!" on the basis of a misreading of the evidence. He was executed, even though the verdict passed on Him was "Innocent!"

Even from the point of view of the human drama of the situation, there is high tension here, a clash between two worlds. As the narrative moves inexorably toward the crucifixion of Jesus, condemned for blasphemy and treason, a mounting chorus of voices maintains His innocence and integrity until, at last, a solitary *Roman* figure appears on center stage to summarize everything that has been said: "He is innocent! This is a righteous man."

Why does this watermark lie on the pages on which the story of Jesus' passion is told?

Why is so much attention paid to the fact that Jesus was accused of the particular crimes of blasphemy and treason?

And why, when both charges were demonstrably false and could not stand up in a court of law, was Jesus not released?

Why was He executed for crimes He never committed?

THE CHRIST?

Actually, raising these questions is the whole point of the narrative. This becomes clear when we notice an earlier identity inquiry in the passage: "If You are the Christ," they said, "tell us" (Luke 22:67).

Jesus was asked: "Are you the Son of God?" The answer was "Yes."

He was asked: "Are you a King?" Again the answer was "Yes."

But the first question was, "Are You the Christ?"

Christ is not part of Jesus' proper name. It is a title, the Greek translation of the Hebrew word *Messiah*, "the person who has been anointed"—in this case, the person anointed by God. "Jesus Christ" means "Jesus the Messiah" or "Jesus the Anointed of God."

In the Old Testament period, God broke through to His people from time to time with pictures and illustrations of the work He eventually would do in

Jesus Christ. He gave prophets to speak His Word to them, high priests who, among other things, offered sacrifices for their sins, and kings who directed them as a nation in the ways of the Lord. All of these were anointed with oil as a symbol that God had called them to a special ministry on behalf of His people.

Jesus is the Christ; He fulfills all three of these roles. The ultimate role of the prophets, priests, and kings was not merely to minister to their contemporaries but to point them forward to Christ—who Himself would be the very Word of God, who would offer the ultimate sacrifice that would take away sin, namely Himself, and who would be the Monarch whose kingdom would never end.

Such a person had been promised in the Old Testament—a prophet greater than Moses (Deut. 18:15–19), a priest after the order of Melchizedek (Ps. 110:4), a king who would reign forever as the Son of David (Ps. 2:6). Jesus is the promised Messiah, the Christ.

So as Luke weaves his verbal tapestry portraying Jesus' passion before our eyes, we begin to see what was really happening. Contrary to what those who wanted to destroy Jesus thought they were doing, they were themselves caught up in the purposes of God to bring salvation to sinners through His Son (Acts 2:23).

Before their blinded eyes, Jesus was fulfilling His messianic ministry.

Prophet, Priest, and King

Notice how all of this emerges. The men who were guarding Jesus began mocking and beating Him. They blindfolded Him and demanded: "Prophesy! Who is the one who struck you?" (Luke 22:64). They played with Jesus: "Prophet! Prophet! If you are a prophet, prophesy!"

Then, as Jesus' passion progressed, Herod and his soldiers also ridiculed and mocked Him. They dressed Him in an elegant, regal robe, then sent Him back to Pilate (23:6–12). It was as if they were saying, "If you are a king, you should be dressed like a king."

Then, as people sneered at Him and mocked Him during His crucifixion, one of the criminals crucified beside Jesus said, "If You are the Christ, save Yourself and us" (23:39).

That was the specific task of the high priest. That was his unique and supreme ministry on Yom Kippur, the annual Day of Atonement. He made sacrifices for the forgiveness of his own sins and then took sacrificial blood into the Holy of Holies—the holiest place of all, so sacred that it was entered only once a year, and then by only one man. On that sacred day, he would sprinkle the blood of a sacrificed animal on the symbolic throne of God on earth and pray for the forgiveness of the people. He entered the presence of God that day to "save others," endangering his own life as he did so (Ex. 28:35).

So when the dying thief turned to Jesus and said, "If You are the Christ, then be the Great High Priest—save Yourself and others," he did not realize that saving others was precisely what Jesus was doing. To do that, He had to lose His own life.

They mocked Him as though He were not a true a prophet. But soon Jesus would turn to the dying thief who said, "Lord, remember me when You come into Your kingdom" (Luke 23:42). He would speak to him with the majesty and authority of the final and true Prophet: "Assuredly, I say to you, today you will be with Me in Paradise."

That dying thief saw something that nobody else had eyes to see. He saw that Jesus was the King, and that His kingdom would extend beyond the death of both of them.

He was indeed the Christ.

In the last hours of Jesus' life, the whole land became dark. The Gospel writers simply note the fact without comment or explanation. The event may have reminded them of more than one significant event in the past. One of them surely would have been the Day of Atonement, when the high priest moved from the outer courts of the temple into the darkness of the hidden, inner room of the Holy of Holies in order to sacrifice and pray for the people. In that hidden room, the sun never shone. The great sacrifice was offered to God far from prying eyes.

On the day of Jesus' crucifixion, the whole land was turned into the Holy of Holies where Jesus the High Priest made not the annual but the final sacrifice for sins. The symbolism was fulfilled in the reality. Thus, the symbol itself was no longer needed. The great curtain in the temple was suddenly torn in two—from the top to the bottom (Luke 22:45). The way to God was now open. God Himself deconsecrated the temple in this dramatic way.

Jesus really was the High Priest. All earlier high priests were mere pictures, actors in a lengthy drama communicating a message to those who watched, pointing forward to the One who was to come and revealing Him to those who had eyes to see. Jesus Himself was the reality. Unlike the earlier sacrificial dramas, this time the High Priest went into the immediate presence of God. On the altar of Calvary, He shed His own blood. Because His was the real sacrifice, God confirmed that it was acceptable to Him by desecrating the temple from heaven. It was as if He were saying "This is not needed any longer." He destroyed the old order. It had served its purpose.

At the Cross

As the drama continued to unfold, there was a further surprise.

Crucifixion was a horrible death. It was a slow death. Men eventually died by asphyxiation. As they weakened, they could no longer raise their bodies sufficiently to make breathing possible. Yet we read of Jesus crying out with a loud voice (Luke 23:46). Was this only a great final effort on His part?

In addition, Jesus appears to have died long before He was expected to (John 19:31–33). Is Luke drawing our attention to the fact that Jesus *chose* the moment of His death—that, in a special sense, He died deliberately, sovereignly, and actively? It seems He chose the moment with regal authority, calling out with a loud voice, "Father, into Your hands I commit My spirit" (23:46). Then He bowed His kingly head and breathed His last.

In Luke's account of the crucifixion, it is fascinating to notice the frequency with which the word *save* is used. "He *saved* others; let Him *save* Himself" (23:35). "*Save* Yourself" (23:36). "*Save* Yourself and us" (23:39).

Luke was not an eyewitness of the Gospel events. He was a later convert to Christianity. But he tells us that he made every effort to speak to eyewitnesses (Luke 1:1–4). He was like an investigative reporter. He took down what these eyewitnesses said. As he listened, he began to see a picture developing—an amazing picture. At the cross, the word that was most frequently on peoples' lips, even in abusive statements, was the key to everything that was happening. The One who was being despised as Prophet, as Priest, and as King actually was God's Prophet, Priest, and King—the Christ, the Savior. He was actually doing what they were cynically calling out for Him to do. They, however, spoke in ignorance; they did not understand that if He was to save others, He could not save Himself.

Here, then, is the mystery of the cross, its whole secret.

Criminal Testimony

Few grasped the secret. One was a Jewish criminal who recognized that this crucified Jesus was none other than the King: "Lord, remember me when You come into Your kingdom," he said. What could he contribute to his salvation? He had nothing but need. But that is all it takes if it brings us to Jesus, the Prophet, Priest, and King, the Savior who died on the cross for our sins.

> There is a fountain filled with blood
> Drawn from Immanuel's veins;
> And sinners plunged beneath that flood,
> Lose all their guilty stains.
>
> The dying thief rejoiced to see
> That fountain in his day;
> And there have I, as vile as he,
> Washed all my sins away.[17]

Near this Jewish criminal who saw that Jesus was the King stood an officer in the Roman army. Had he earlier joined in the mockery of Jesus with his subordinates? Possibly, since we know that "the soldiers also mocked Him" (Luke 23:36). But now he recognized that Jesus was the Righteous One (23:47). Why, then, was He suffering this punishment? Again the question is pressed on us by the narrative Luke unfolds. This One—we are being led to understand—must be suffering because of the unrighteousness of others. But whose?

Is it possible that this Roman officer might have been able to take these words on his lips?

Behold the Man upon a cross,
My sin upon His shoulders.
Ashamed, I hear my mocking voice
Call out among the scoffers.

It was my sin that held Him there
Until it was accomplished.
His dying breath has brought me life.
I know that it is finished.[18]

Blasphemy and Treason

The two charges leveled against Jesus were blasphemy (that He had made Himself equal with God) and treason (that He had rejected lawfully constituted authority).

Why were those two charges so significant? It was because these are the charges each of us faces before the judgment seat of God.

In that court, I am guilty of blasphemy, because I have made myself rather than God the center of the universe.

I am also guilty of treason, since I have sought to overturn His lawfully and graciously constituted authority over my life.

Blasphemy and treason were also the crimes of Adam. These are the age-old crimes of which every one of us—old and young, rich and poor, wise and simple, famous and infamous—stands accused. We are on the same charge sheet. We are all guilty.

But Jesus has come!

Bearing shame and scoffing rude,
In my place condemned he stood,
Sealed my pardon with his blood:
Hallelujah! What a Savior![19]

How well this is expressed in Christopher Idle's words:

He stood before the court,
On trial instead of us;
He met its power to hurt,
Condemned to face the cross.
Our King, accused of treachery;
Our God, abused for blasphemy![20]

Jesus came and suffered all this to take our place, to bear our judgment, to deal with our sin, and to save us.

All this we see in the intricate weaving of Luke's tapestry portraying Jesus' passion. The central motif is now clear: Jesus Christ died for sinners, the Just for the unjust, to bring us to God (1 Peter 3:18).

The meaning of the cross is this: "While we were still sinners, Christ died for us" (Rom. 5:8).

He took my place. I take His grace. He becomes my Savior.

Is that true for you?

Not for my righteousness,
For I have none,
But for his mercy's sake,
Jesus, God's Son,
Suffered on Calvary's tree—
Crucified with thieves was he—

Are you able to sing?

Great was his grace to me,
His wayward one.

4

And when I think of how,
At Calvary,
He bore sin's penalty
Instead of me,
Amazed, I wonder why
He, the sinless One, should die
For one so vile as I;
My Saviour he!

Chapter Four

A GREAT EXCHANGE

One hundred and four men have been archbishops of Canterbury. In the year 1093, one of the greatest of them wrote a book that ranks among the most influential works of theology ever penned. He was an Italian whose name was Anselm.

Anselm was a medieval figure. He is sometimes described as "The Father of Medieval Scholasticism"—a way of thinking and studying used in the various "schools" of learning in medieval Europe that served as forerunners of the university. Not surprisingly, since he wrote in Latin, Anselm gave his great book a Latin title: *Cur Deus Homo*, that is, *Why the God-Man?* Or perhaps, *Why Did God Become Man?*

It is a great title. Three simple Latin words (*Why*, *God*, and *Man*) take us to the most important question in the Bible.

This is the question at the heart of the wonder E. T. Sibomana expresses:

And when I think of how,
At Calvary,
He bore sin's penalty
Instead of me,

Amazed, I wonder why
He, the sinless One, should die
For one so vile as I;
My Saviour he!

Several passages in the New Testament answer Anselm's question and explain Pastor Sibomana's amazement. Among them is 2 Corinthians 5.

The gospel is an invitation to receive a gift. But many people hear it as a summons to do better. Paul makes it clear that the gospel is not about something we do. It is about what God has done for us in Jesus Christ.

The human predicament is multifaceted. The gospel is as multifaceted. It needs to be in order to save us.

Paul sometimes uses the language of the law court. We are guilty, but by God's grace we can be justified.

At other times, he uses the language of the temple. We are not fit to come into the presence of a holy God, but in His mercy, He has provided a way for our sins to be covered and for His face to be uncovered in grace to us.

On other occasions, Paul employs the language of the ancient market, where men and women were bound in slavery and put up for sale to the highest bidder. Paul explains how Jesus Christ came into the slave market and, through His death on the cross, paid the redemption price that set us free from our bondage in sin.

Each of these aspects of Christ's ministry helps us answer Anselm's question, "Why did God become man?" Christ came to bring justification, to make propitiation, and to effect redemption.

But Paul has yet another aspect to unfold: reconciliation. It belongs to the world of fractured relationships—of alienation.

This is the language of our times. We live in a world of broken relationships. We have individuals and organizations in our society whose sole function is to heal alienation and to bring about reconciliation.

Here, then, is a further way to help us understand what Jesus Christ has done.

THE BASIC PROBLEM

Alienation was one of the "buzz words" of the twentieth century and a key idea in Marxist communism.

Karl Marx held that a fundamental problem with the world was the deep alienation between the working classes and the fruits of their labor. He believed that if only we could set the worker free to enjoy ownership in his labor, a foundational element of the world's ills would be dissipated. This was part of the central message of communism.

Marx failed to take account of what became obvious behind the iron and bamboo curtains: human greed, pride, and the lust for power. It became increasingly clear in communist states that there was deep-dyed and high-reaching corruption. Instead of bringing reconciliation, communism simply continued to sustain human sinfulness. Alienation remained.

With the rise of psychiatry and psychology, not least in their "pop" versions, we have now become a therapeutic culture—patients who need inner healing, victims who need a better self-image. Our deepest problem is now seen to be personal alienation—whether from those around us or from ourselves. Thus, many therapists set out to deal with those alienations as if they were "sicknesses" without any moral dimension, behavior patterns for which the individual bears no personal moral responsibility.

In so many instances, however, this is what the philosophers call a "category mistake." It treats as illness behavior patterns that properly belong to the category of moral disorder. It should not surprise us that such therapy cannot solve the world's ills. Neither should we expect it to. Therapy that takes no account of man's deepest problem—sin—can never resolve man's deepest alienation—his broken relationship with God.

A socioeconomic theory cannot bring world-scale or individual reconciliation when the basic problem is moral. Treating sinful behavior as a medical category and prescribing chemical therapy will not solve alienations that are not caused by chemical deficiency. The problem is not ultimately economic, biological, or chemical.

In 2 Corinthians 5, Paul squarely faces the basic problem. He deals with the mother alienation that gives birth to all other alienations: the alienation between God and man, man and God. His desire is to explain the divine remedy for it.

But first we need to consider why this reconciliation is so necessary.

Distorted Design

Christians no longer live for themselves (2 Cor. 5:15). The implication is that before we become Christians, we *do* live this way. Our worldview is self-focused. Man is, in Martin Luther's words, "*incurvatus in se*"—turned in on himself, self-obsessed. We belong to what Christopher Lasch has called a culture of narcissism.[21] All this stands in sharp contrast with the divine design, which is—as the famous words of the Westminster Shorter Catechism put it—that we should glorify God and enjoy Him forever.

So we are seriously adrift. We have distorted God's original design.

Contemporary men and women find it almost impossible to conceive that they were made to glorify *and* to enjoy God. It would perhaps be more accurate to say that the very idea of living for the glory of God appears to be many people's idea of hell. We might rework the famous words in Jean-Paul Sartre's play *No Exit*, "Hell is other people." To many, hell is the presence of God. But to live for ourselves, that is heaven.

Or is it?

Tragically, instead of finding profound and lasting pleasure in God's world, we find only increased alienation there.

Alienation from God is not only real but dangerous—and the depth of the alienation is evidenced by the fact that we think we are in no danger at all. The sobering truth, however, is that "We must all appear before the judgment seat of Christ, that each one may receive the things done in the body, according to what he has done, whether good or bad" (2 Cor. 5:10).

The average person finds this analysis distasteful. He is, in his own view, far from being alienated from God. But there are simple tests for this alienation. Mention the words "the Lord Jesus Christ" and watch the reaction; it may vary from an embarrassed silence to a violent argument. Why this response? The New Testament indicates that God's great purpose is that we should honor His Son. Therefore, *not* to honor Him is, surely, to be deeply alienated from Him.

So when Paul speaks about the need for the gospel in this way, he hits the nail on the head. If reminding people that they are by nature alienated from God arouses hostility in them, no further proof of their alienation is needed.

But Paul also knows that the gospel perfectly fits the human condition. We are warped and twisted in our alienation from God. The gospel tells us that Jesus Christ came to replace that alienation with reconciliation.

Paul uses the language of reconciliation several times in 2 Corinthians 5 (vv. 18, 19, 20, 21). He is an ambassador of Jesus Christ with a marvelous message: God was in Christ reconciling the world to Himself. We are now called to be reconciled to God—to give up our resistance and to yield to Him.

This sounds more like a sermon for the marketplace rather than for the local church in Corinth. Yet Paul is preaching to Christians. It is as if he were saying to them: "What you need to hear most of all is the gospel, and the gospel that you need to hear is the same gospel I preach out there in the marketplace." He understands that our greatest need, whether we are Christians or not, is to respond to the gospel. So whether he is speaking to non-Christians or to Christians, he is unashamed to say to them, "Understand this, respond to God's saving grace in Christ, and life will be transformed."

But how is this reconciliation to take place?

THE EXCHANGE

Reconciliation is provided for us in Jesus Christ: "God was in Christ reconciling the world to Himself" (2 Cor. 5:19). How did that happen? Paul explains: "He [God] made Him [Christ] who knew no sin to be sin for us, that we might become the righteousness of God in Him" (v. 21).

Notice that Paul does not say that God reconciled the world to Himself by Jesus becoming flesh for us. We are not reconciled by Christmas. The incarnation is essential, but it is only the beginning of the story. God reconciled the world to Himself *by Jesus becoming sin for us.*

These words are the core of the gospel. They describe not only how God made His Son to be sin for us, but also how those who trust in His Son become the righteousness of God. Truly this is an unexpected change of places—a mysterious but marvelous exchange:

- Jesus Christ, who knew no sin, became sin for us.
- We, who knew no righteousness, become, in Christ, the righteousness of God.

The word for "reconciliation" in the New Testament (Greek, *katallagē*) has the root idea of "making a change." It was used in the ancient world of exchanging money—you give someone money and he gives you another currency in exchange. Here is the heart of the gospel: in Jesus Christ, God has made a unique exchange. He made Christ to be sin for us; He counts the righteousness of Christ to us.

In Old Testament days, when a man had sinned, he brought an animal to the priest as a sacrifice. Placing his hands on its head, he confessed his sins, symbolically transferring them to the animal. The animal "became sin" for him (although it had no "sin" of its own). The animal was then slain and offered as a sacrifice. This was a powerful visible symbol of the costliness of forgiveness and of reconciliation with God.

It is difficult for us to grasp the impact these sacrifices must have made. They would have affected the people's senses deeply. The animals could be seen and touched. The sound of the animal being executed, the sight of the blood, and the smell of it in the air must have left an indelible impression on anyone who offered a sacrifice.

There were gradations in these sacrifices, of course. Once every year, there was a great day of sacrifice—Yom Kippur, the Day of Atonement—when sacrifice was made for the sins of all the people. Leviticus 16 describes the elaborate ritual that the high priest followed. However, the principle of these sacrifices was always the same. The sins of the people were exchanged for the sacrifice of an innocent animal. The animal was treated as though it were responsible for the people's sins; it bore the judgment of death due to the people for their sins. The people, in turn, were treated in the sight of God as though they were righteous.

Double Agony

Paul saw all this fulfilled in Christ's death on the cross: "He made Him who knew no sin to be sin for us." Christ accepted the judgment against our sin and set us free from its penalty. God treats us now not simply as innocent, but as actually righteous.

Even the details of the Day of Atonement foreshadowed Jesus' later experience. On that day, two goats were selected. Lots were cast to select different roles for each of them.

One goat was slain as a sin offering.

The high priest placed his hands on the other and confessed the sins of the people. They were "put on the head" of the goat (Lev. 16:21). It was led away into the wilderness "to an uninhabited land" (v. 22) and set free to wander there without prospect of return.

Together, these two goats give a vivid picture of what was involved in Jesus being "made sin" for us.

Jesus died for our sin. But there is a dark and lonely dimension to His experience. During His crucifixion, He hung in a wilderness between heaven and earth. He was rejected by humanity and experienced a sense of being forsaken by His Father, forcing from Him the poignant cry, "My God, My God, why have You forsaken Me?" (Matt. 27:46). He experienced *both* the judgment of God against sin and the sense of divine abandonment that it involved. He became both the sacrifice and the scapegoat.

> *O generous love! That He, who smote,*
> *In Man for man the foe,*
> *The double agony in Man*
> *For man should undergo.*[22]

It is essential to grasp Paul's teaching here—whether you are on the margins of the Christian faith or a long-term believer: You did not, do not, and cannot earn your own salvation. You can contribute nothing to it in any way. It is not earned by your achievements, your merit, your faith, your level of sanctification, your faithfulness, or your Christian service.

Reconciliation is a free gift of grace from beginning to end.

Christ already has done everything that is needed in order to take your sins and to transfer His righteousness to you.

Inadequate Sacrifices

Of course, in the last analysis, those Old Testament sacrifices could not take away sins. They were simply pictures, no more.

People understood that in Old Testament times. Having offered their sacrifices on one day, they knew more sacrifices would have to be offered the next day, and the next, and on into the future. Even the great once-a-year sacrifice of the Day of Atonement had to be repeated year after year.

It did not require training in logic to understand that if this was the case, none of these sacrifices was fully and finally taking away sin and guilt.

More than this, Old Testament believers must have seen that the sacrifice of an animal could never be an appropriate, far less adequate, payment for a man's sins. The only possible substitute for a sinful man is a man.

Animal sacrifices pointed to the need for someone to appear who could and would die in the place of sinners—but it had to be someone who required no sacrifice for himself, someone without sin.

But where could a man be found who would be so innocent, so pure, so righteous that he would not need to die for his own sins?

No such person had ever lived, "for all have sinned and fall short of the glory of God" (Rom. 3:23).

So God solved the dilemma by coming Himself, in the person of His Son. He took our human nature in His incarnation in order to bear our sin on the cross. In essence, He exchanged places with us:

Bearing shame and scoffing rude,
In my place condemned he stood,
Sealed my pardon with his blood:
Hallelujah! What a Savior![23]

Yet at the same time, He was a divine person, so His sacrifice was of infinite value and worth. It had the value of the person who made it—the Son of God. It was therefore not merely an adequate sacrifice for the sins of only one individual ("eye for eye, tooth for tooth"; Ex. 21:24) but sufficient for everyone who comes to Christ in faith and says, "You are able to save me; I repent of all the sin that required You to go to the cross as my substitute; I believe on You as my Savior and my Lord."

It is in this way that the reconciliation provided for us in Jesus Christ becomes ours. This is a truly glorious exchange.

THE RELEASE

Reconciliation through Christ releases us from the guilt of sin. Paul affirms that "God was reconciling the world to himself in Christ, not counting men's sins against them . . ." (2 Cor. 5:19, NIV).

We may have encountered non-Christians who say: "This is exactly what I have advocated. That's the kind of God I believe in—a God who doesn't count men's sins. You have gone on and on about my sins—but your own Bible says God doesn't count them. This is exactly my own conviction. Don't you believe your own Bible? Here is your great apostle Paul teaching exactly what I believe—God doesn't count sins. That's the kind of God I believe in!"

But the unbeliever is not reading Paul's words properly, is he?

Paul *does* say that God did not count men's sins against them. But it would be a fatal mistake to leave it at that. We need to read his words with greater care.

Paul assumes that God *does* count men's sins. He has already said that we must all appear before the judgment seat of Christ to receive what we are due for what we have done, whether good or bad (v. 10). Sins *will* be counted.

Notice, too, that Paul says God was making this reconciliation "in Christ." Paul says: God does not count sins *against those who believe in Christ.*

Against whom, then, does God count sins?

He counts them *against His Son, Jesus Christ.*

This is the heart of the gospel. God's Son became flesh so that He might then become our sin. As if He were Himself a sinner, Christ—who "knew no sin"—bore God's judgment (v. 21). His righteousness—worked out in a life in which He kept God's law for us and also through a death in which God judged, condemned, and handed Him over to the executioner for our sakes—becomes ours.

Faith says: "Yes, God counts my sins. But He does not count them against me. Rather, He counts my sins against His Son." When I stretch out the empty hands of faith and take hold of Jesus Christ, in that very moment the sacrifice of Jesus Christ becomes mine, and in that same moment I am released from the guilt and bondage of sin.

A Legal Standing

Guilt is not just a feeling. It is not just a psychological condition, although it can become one. It is a legal standing.

When the foreman of the jury in a trial speaks the word *Guilty*, he is not commenting on the feelings of the accused. He is pronouncing a verdict. He is saying that the accused has been judged to have committed the crimes with which he was charged. The accused is guilty and will be treated accordingly—no matter what he or she may "feel."

Whether people feel guilty is not really the issue. My feelings, or lack of them, neither increase nor lessen my guilt. It is first and foremost a personal standing before a holy God, not a psychological condition.

The marvel of the gospel is that it deals with our objective guilt. Then we begin to appreciate our new standing before God. At that point, God begins to transform our feelings.

The stories of how individuals are converted vary enormously, but there is one strand that features constantly. They may have begun with no obvious awareness of guilt and no special sense of need for God. When probed a little, they might have been self-defensive, even self-justifying, but nevertheless they felt secure, safe.

But nobody can protect himself or herself fully and finally from God's invasions.

God often creates a sense of unease in people, which then leads them to a consciousness of sin, and then a deeper sense that they are guilty before God. Then He brings them beyond mere "feelings" of guilt to confess, "*I am guilty before God.*" As the psalmist says, "If You, LORD, should mark iniquities, O Lord, who could stand?" (Ps. 130:3).

Then God's Spirit brings us to faith in Christ. We see that He has taken the penalty for our sin. Our guilt is removed. We are pardoned. As we begin to understand the gospel better, the knowledge that we are no longer guilty begins to pervade our spirits and to influence our feelings. We are set free from both the guilt of sin and the guiltiness we feel in our consciences because of it. We can now begin to live in the presence of God. More than that, He welcomes us as His sons and His daughters.

Do you see what true spiritual therapy this is? The divine Counselor does not say to the person who feels guilt for sin, "You don't need to worry about this." That would be a counsel of despair. Such words have no power.

But when you say to someone who feels guilty, "You *are* guilty; you *really are* guilty," then you also can say, "But there is a way in which your guilt can be dealt with."

No therapist, no psychiatrist can relieve you of guilt. He or she may help you to resolve feelings of false guilt that can arise for a variety of reasons. Prescription drugs may provide certain kinds of ease. But no therapy, no course of drugs, can deliver you from real guilt. Why? Because being guilty is not a medical condition or a chemical disorder. It is a spiritual reality. It concerns your standing before God. The psychiatrist cannot forgive you; the therapist cannot absolve you; the counselor cannot pardon you.

But the message of the gospel is this: *God* can forgive you, and He is willing to do so.

First, however, you need to be brought to the place where you say, "I am guilty."

Is your response one of self-justification, even of anger? "How dare anybody say to me, 'You are guilty'!"

Does that apply even if the one saying so is God?

Until we acknowledge our sin and guilt, we will never come to discover that it can be forgiven. But when we do, actual forgiveness begins to give rise to an awareness of forgiveness psychologically, spiritually, mentally, inwardly. With that comes an increasing sense that the bondage of guilt has been broken. At last, we are set free. Wonder of wonders, we discover that at the very heart of the gospel is this fact: God has taken our guilt upon Himself in His Son Jesus Christ.

Covenant Grace

After the judgment of the flood, God made His covenant with Noah and symbolized it with the rainbow in the sky (Gen. 9:8–17). Old Testament scholars have sometimes suggested that the rainbow is a multicolored bow of war that God has symbolically flung into the sky. If so, its deadly arrow points *heavenward*. Any arrow of judgment will be fired directly into the heart of God Himself. That is a hint of things to come.

When God made His covenant with Abraham, He moved as a light between two parallel lines of slain animals (Gen. 15). God said, symbolically, to Abraham, "If it costs Me My existence to bring this covenant promise of blessing to pass, I will pay that price."

That is the heart of the gospel. That is the reason why God became man. That is the meaning of Jesus' life and ministry. That is the significance of the cross. The arrow of God's judgment against our sin penetrated the heart of God Himself on Calvary. As He brought His covenant pledge to fulfillment, God Himself took our guilt and its judgment. The cross says: "I am bearing the penalty of your guilt Myself, and I will set you free from its bondage and from its power."

It is a wonderful moment when this dawns on us. Yes, people take different lengths of time before this truth really permeates every part of their lives. But this is the truth of the gospel: the moment you trust in Jesus Christ, your sins are forgiven and your guilt is removed.

THE TRANSFORMATION

So reconciliation is provided in Christ. It releases us from the guilt of sin. But it also transforms the whole of life: "He made Him who knew no sin to be sin for us, *that we might become the righteousness of God in Him*" (2 Cor. 5:21, emphasis added).

Can we really be righteous in God's sight? Yes, but the truth is even more remarkable—in Jesus Christ, I am as righteous in God's sight as Jesus Christ Himself. How can that be?

The only righteousness with which I am righteous is Jesus Christ's righteousness. It is as if He has said to me: "Here is my righteousness. Wear it; it is yours. It fits your needs perfectly and completely." As I stand in God's presence and He looks at me, I hear Him say: "Where have I seen that righteousness before? Come near. I recognize it now. That is My Son's righteousness you are wearing. Enter! You are welcome—and safe—here."

But that is only the beginning of the transformation. Paul takes us a step further: "Therefore, if anyone is in Christ, he is a new creation" (2 Cor. 5:17a), literally, "If anyone in Christ—new creation." Strictly speaking you do not become a "new creature" (as older versions translated it). You remain a human being. But when you become a Christian, you are united to Christ ("in Christ"), and through Christ the Door (John 10:9), you enter into a new order of existence, a whole new world.

New Creation
New life in Christ involves more than an individual transformation. Everything about life becomes new. Everything changes. Why? Because you now stand in a new place. You breathe new air. You see everything through new eyes. You are given a new heart. You have been brought into a new community. You have a

new purpose. You have a new—and glorious—destiny. You have entered into a new creation altogether. "Old things have passed away; behold, all things have become new" (2 Cor. 5:17b).

The exchange on the cross of Calvary is the fundamental exchange. But it is also the beginning of exchanges. As George Wade Robinson puts it:

Heav'n above is softer blue,
Earth around is sweeter green,
Something lives in every hue
Christless eyes have never seen.[24]

This transformation then begins to work deep down into your life. "Even though we have known Christ according to the flesh [i.e., from a this-worldly point of view], yet now we know Him thus no longer" (2 Cor. 5:16).

That is the first and most immediate thing: we have a different view of Jesus because He is Lord and Savior. We love Him. We trust Him. We sense His presence. We know His power. We see His direction. We live for His praise. He has become our Master. The old has gone, the new has come. There has been an exchange.

But there is a further dimension to this exchange—a new attitude toward self: "He [Christ] died for all, that those who live [because He died] should live no longer for themselves, but for Him who died for them and rose again" (2 Cor. 5:15). You used to live for yourself, but now you live for Christ. Your own desires and plans are secondary. Christ's will, Christ's desires, Christ's glory—these are now primary.

But there is more—a new attitude to other people: "Therefore [notice that Paul sees this as a spiritual and logical implication of the gospel], from now on, we regard no one according to the flesh [i.e., from a this-worldly point of view]," (2 Cor. 5:16). We see people as though we looked at them through the eyes of our Lord Jesus Christ. How marvelous!

Consider, for example, a young person who has come to a living faith in Jesus Christ. The exchange that Christ has made *for* her begins to produce a change *in* her. Her parents are perhaps not Christians. But now she no longer speaks of her parents in the way others do. Her disposition toward her father and mother has changed. She begins to love her parents, to care for them, to pray for them.

Isn't that something—a teenage girl who prays day by day, night by night, for her mom and her dad, because she longs to see them come to know what she has come to know in Jesus Christ? This is a new order of reality, a new world altogether.

All of this, says Paul, comes from God (2 Cor. 5:18). He gives and keeps on giving. The evidence that we have received His gifts is that this great exchange has taken place in our lives.

The Day of Salvation

This is why Paul sounds as though he is speaking in the marketplace to non-Christians. There is a great sense of urgency in his voice: "We are ambassadors for Christ, as though God were pleading through us [which, in reality, He is]. We implore you on Christ's behalf, be reconciled to God" (2 Cor. 5:20). In other words: "Come to Christ. Trust in Christ. Give yourself to Christ. Turn away from the old by God's grace and experience new life in Christ, who makes everything new."

Those who made the original chapter divisions in our Bibles seem to have obscured the point Paul is making here. Second Corinthians 6:1–2 really forms the conclusion to what Paul says in chapter 5: "We then, as workers together with Him also plead with you not to receive the grace of God in vain. For He says: 'In an acceptable time I have heard you, and in the day of salvation I have helped you.' Behold, now is the accepted time; behold, now is the day of salvation."

Why is there such urgency? Paul had often seen signs of the interest in the gospel that the Spirit of God creates. But he had seen people brought face to face with Jesus Christ only to say, "I'll decide about that later." Many today do the same. They pass by the day of opportunity. Later, they look back and say, "I wonder why I saw anything in that Christian gospel?" Then their hearts become hardened all over again.

You may have been going to church for years, or perhaps just been on the margins. You might even have thought you were a Christian. Perhaps no one who knows you has ever doubted that you are a Christian. But it has become clear to you that you have been simply following a formula. It may even be an evangelical formula. But it is no more than a formula. Trusting and knowing Christ are not realities to you.

It would be the easiest thing in the world to say, "If that's really true, I'll need to think more seriously about it—but on another day." But it may be now or never.

Perhaps this is "the day." It is really *now* or it may indeed be *never*. God has been speaking to you. The issue could not be clearer to you than it has become in recent days. Your greatest need is to have your sin and your guilt exchanged for pardon and new life. On the cross, Jesus has taken our sin, and He offers Himself to us as Savior. You must take hold of Him in faith and say, "Lord Jesus, I confess I really am a sinner."

You may be a twenty-year-old sinner or a sixty-year-old sinner. It makes no difference to Him. Simply say to Him: "Lord Jesus, I am a sinner, and I know that I need Your grace and Your forgiveness. I need the exchange that You alone can offer me." As you do, He will take you by the hand and draw you to Himself. Even if you say to Him, "Lord Jesus, I don't really know if I can trust You," He will say, "Trust Me, trust Me." Trust Him, and you will find that all your guilt will be gone. You will have stepped through the Door into a new creation altogether.

Some experience this suddenly and dramatically. Some experience it slowly and almost imperceptibly.

But Christ offers Himself freely to all who will come to Him and place their trust in Him.

Do not put Him off when He speaks to you in His Word.

Pastor Sibomana was right to express amazement at the great exchange that took place at Calvary:

Amazed, I wonder why
He, the sinless One, should die

For one so vile as I;
My Saviour he.

Does this amaze you?
Can you say with Pastor Sibomana, "My Saviour he"?

5

————

Now all my heart's desire
Is to abide
In him, my Saviour dear,
In him to hide.
My shield and buckler he,
Covering and protecting me;
From Satan's darts I'll be
Safe at his side.

Chapter Five

GUARANTEED SECURITY

You would not expect a non-Christian to find the grace of God amazing. Sadly, we Christians, who sing about "amazing grace," sometimes lose sight and sense of its graciousness. It ceases to amaze us. To the extent this is true, we have lost our grip on the gospel of Jesus Christ. We need to rediscover how amazing the grace of God is.

E. T. Sibomana's Burundi hymn, "O How the Grace of God Amazes Me," has an unusual structure. It begins by reflecting on the way in which the grace of God sets us free from spiritual bondage: "It loosed me from my bonds and set me free!"

It then encourages us to sing about the greatest of our spiritual privileges—that we are adopted into God's family: "O, the love that made him run to meet his erring son!"

In the next two verses, we are taken to the heart and root of the gospel and to the source of these spiritual blessings: Jesus Christ, our crucified and risen Savior.

But then, perhaps surprisingly, we come to two verses that focus on the testing and trials of the Christian life. Here we are introduced to the grace of God in the context of a spiritual battle where we encounter "Satan's darts" and "Satan's art." We need protection:

My shield and buckler he,
Covering and protecting me;
From Satan's darts I'll be
Safe at his side.

Dangerous Territory

As soon as we come to Christ, we find ourselves in territory that is full of hidden mines—sinister explosive devices planted by a malignant hand in an attempt to destroy our Christian faith.

Of course, Satan can attack but never ultimately destroy true Christian faith, because we are preserved by grace. Therefore, he seeks to destroy our *enjoyment* of the grace of God. In this, sadly, he frequently succeeds.

One of the ways in which he does this is by "the fiery darts" with which he attacks the Christian.

This language, of course, is drawn from Paul's words in Ephesians:

Put on the whole armor of God, that you may be able to stand against the wiles of the devil. For we do not wrestle against flesh and blood, but against principalities, against powers, against the rulers of the darkness of this age, against spiritual hosts of wickedness in the heavenly places. Therefore take up the whole armor of God, that you may be able to withstand in the evil day, and having done all, to stand. Stand therefore, having girded your waist with truth, having put on the breastplate of righteousness, and having shod your feet with the preparation of the gospel of peace; above all, taking the shield of faith with which you will be able to quench *all the fiery darts of the evil one.* (Eph. 6:11–16, emphasis added)

The Christian needs the "shield of faith" for protection against Satan's darts. Paul's word here for "shield" (*thureos*) comes from the Greek word for a door (*thura*). It refers to the long, oblong shield Roman soldiers carried into battle for whole-body protection. It was more than four feet long and two feet wide.

These shields were deployed in different ways. One technique was to dampen the shields so that blazing arrows fired against them would be quenched. The opening moments of the movie *Gladiator* vividly portray such a scene—arrows with tips dipped in pitch and set ablaze shot toward enemy forces, creating panic in the ranks in order to put them to flight.

Paul makes use of this picture when he describes the Christian's spiritual armor. Clearly he is not thinking about the Roman soldier who is standing guard over him in prison—although he is indeed behind bars. Soldiers assigned to such duty did not normally carry the equivalent of a small door! Rather, in his mind's eye, Paul sees a Roman soldier on the battlefield, kitted out for action.

Jesus builds His church on enemy-occupied territory (Matt. 16:18). The Christian lives on a battlefield. He or she is exposed to the attacks of the Evil One. But the gospel provides marvelous defensive armor that can withstand all of Satan's opposition.

The "What" and the "How"

It is one thing for us to know that God Himself is a shield for His people (Pss. 3:3; 33:20). It is another thing for us to know how to use "the shield of faith" that God gives to His people for their protection. Knowledge always needs to be translated into wisdom. It is not enough for me to know the answers to the big theological questions that all begin with "What": "What is this? What is that? What is the truth about this? What is the shield of faith?" Such knowledge is of little value unless it also helps us to answer the "How" questions: "How does this work out in my life? How do I do it?"

Precisely here the apostle Paul is a help to us. In Romans 8:28, he affirms that all things "work together" for the good of believers, since we have been "called according to His purpose." God has an invincible plan. Those He foreknew, He predestined. Those He predestined, He called. Those He called, He justified. Those He justified, He glorified (vv. 29–30). This is God's certain plan. It is unchangeable, invincible.

But even though we know this, it may make no difference to the way we live. There is, as John Owen liked to say, a difference between the knowledge of the truth and the knowledge of the power of the truth. We can possess factual knowledge about the character of God—that He is a shield—and yet lack confidence in His protection.

The real question for Paul—and for us—is not, "Is God able to keep His people secure?" It is, "How is God going to keep me secure?" Not, "Do I know what God's plan is?" but, "What practical difference does it make to my life to know that God has a plan?" Not, "What do I know?" but, "How do I put into action what I know?"

When Paul turns from Romans 8:28–30 to 8:31–39, he begins to answer these questions.

We can express this in another way. Paul believes that the Christian is secure. But he is now asking more penetrating questions: "What does that mean to me when I feel as though all hell is breaking loose in an assault against my soul? What do I do then? How do I use the truth that God has revealed to me in order to stand in the evil day? How does God, in practical terms, keep me secure when the fiery darts of Satan are aimed at me and heading toward me?"

It is just here that the questions asked in Romans 8:31–35 have great significance.

Paul begins by asking a "What" question: "What then shall we say to these things?" (v. 31a). But from that point onward, his questions all employ the *personal* interrogative "Who":

- Verse 31b: "*Who* can be against us?"
- Verse 33: "*Who* shall bring any charge against God's elect?"
- Verse 34a: "*Who* is he who condemns?"
- Verse 35a: "*Who* shall separate us from the love of Christ?"

Paul is not asking, "*What* is going to provide the opposition to my perseverance in the Christian life?" He is asking, "*Who* is going to do this?"

Why does he ask his questions in this way?

The answer is that Paul knows the identity of the "Who." He goes on to mention four of the most powerful fiery darts that Satan aims at Christian believers in order to destroy their enjoyment of the grace of God:

• Fiery Dart 1: "God is against you," Satan says. "He is not really for you. How can you believe He is for you when you see the things that are happening in your life?"

• Fiery Dart 2: "I have accusations I will bring against you because of your sins," Satan argues. "What can you say in your defense? Nothing."

• Fiery Dart 3: "You say you are forgiven, but there is a payback day coming—a condemnation day," Satan insinuates. "How will you defend yourself then?"

• Fiery Dart 4: "Given your track record, what hope is there that you will persevere to the end?" Satan asks.

These four fiery darts hit their targets in the minds and consciences of many Christians. The questions and accusations come unbidden; they become part of our thinking, emerging at the forefront of our minds from who knows where. Many Christians can testify to the unsettling of the heart they produce. Suddenly, our thoughts are aflame with fears and doubts; we lose our hold on peace, joy, and assurance. We lose sight, sense, and sound of the strong word of the gospel, which says there is nothing in all of creation that can ever separate us from the love of God in Jesus Christ.

So when Satan fires his darts against us, what are we to do?

Listen to Paul as he faces down his enemy. Had he also experienced the wounds made by these four darts—perhaps on more than one occasion—as Satan sought to destroy his faith? Surely, for there was much in Paul's past to inflame guilt and fear.

WHO CAN BE AGAINST US?

God has promised to work everything together for the good of His people. If God is for us, it follows that, ultimately, nothing can stand against us. That is logical. Otherwise, God would not be God. If something could rise up against God and overcome Him, that other thing would be God. God would then prove to be a false god—no God at all. But on the contrary Paul is saying that in the last analysis, nothing can be against us if God is for us.

But this raises the million-dollar question: "*Is* God for me?" Perhaps even more pointed is the personal question: "How do I *know* that God is for me?"

Well, do you know that? How do you know?

Satan is very insistent about this—indeed, he has been insistent on this question from the beginning. He asked it in the Garden of Eden. In fact, his first recorded words are an assault on God's gracious character (will we never learn how much he hates God and His people?): "Did God put you in this lavish garden and forbid you to eat from any of its trees? What kind of God does that? You don't think He is really for you, do you, if He does that kind of thing?" (see Gen. 3:1).

You will find this innuendo repeated in various forms and guises throughout your Christian life. You need to have biblical answers to these questions:

• How do you know God is really for you?

• Where should you look for the proof that God is for you? Does it lie in the fact that your Christian life has been unbroken happiness? Does it lie in the fact that your Christian life been one of ecstatic joy?

There is only one irrefutable answer to these questions. It cannot be found in our circumstances. It lies only in the provision that God has made for us in Jesus Christ.

This is the whole point of Paul's question in verse 32. We can be sure that God is for us because this God, the God of the Bible, the God and Father of our Lord Jesus Christ, did not spare His own Son, but gave Him up to the cross for us all.

If this is true, Paul affirms, we can be confident He will give us everything we will ever need.

This is the only sure way we can know that God is for us.

Frequently in the closing pages of the Gospel records we are told that the Lord Jesus Christ was "delivered up" (e.g., Matt. 26:15; 27:2, 18, 26). He was handed over by one person or group to another until eventually He was handed over by Pilate to be crucified as a criminal.

But Paul understood that behind every human "handing over" was the purpose of the heavenly Father. He "handed over" (it is the same verb) His own Son to bear the condemnation due to sinners.

Here is the heart of the plan of God and the wonder of the gospel. The best of all men dies as though He were the worst of all criminals. This is not merely a matter of human wickedness destroying a good man. It is the heart of the purpose of God, as Isaiah had long before prophesied (Isa. 53:4–6, 10).

Behind the handing over of the Lord Jesus—by Judas Iscariot, by Herod, by the priests, by Pontius Pilate—stood the purposes of His heavenly Father handing Him over to the cross in order to die in the place of sinners. He bore God's judgment and wrath against our sin.

What inexpressible love this is.

A Powerful Implication

Paul insists that Christians learn to think clearly, to draw logical deductions from the gospel. Therefore, he points here to a powerful practical implication of the cross: God can point us to the cross and say:

- "Do you see how much I love you?"
- "I was prepared to bear My own judgment against your sin in the person of My own Son."
- "If I was prepared to do that for you, there is nothing I will withhold from you for your good."

You will never understand the heart of God until you understand this.

If we want to know God and to hear His heartbeat for us, we must realize that His Son died on the cross for us. It is as if God Himself says to us: "If you want to know Me and to understand My commitment to save and bless you; if you want to be sure of the privileges that are yours and the security I have provided for you; then you must not look first at the circumstances of your life and conclude, 'Things are going well for me, God must love me.' No. You must look at the cross and say: 'My God was willing to give His Son for me. That is why I know He loves me.'"

The only way you can really feel the security of God's love is by beginning to understand the inner meaning of the death of Jesus on the cross. Rather than abandon you to His judgment against your sin, God bore that judgment Himself—if I may put this reverently—in the loss of His own Son.

Paul says that he is prepared to "count all things loss for the excellence of the knowledge of Christ Jesus my Lord" (Phil. 3:8). We can also say that the heavenly Father was prepared to count everything as loss. He was prepared to count His own Son as loss in order that we might know His love and grace toward us.

As this fiery dart comes toward Paul—"How do you really know God loves you?"—his answer is not, "I deserve to be loved." Neither is it, "Things are going so well in my life it is obvious that God loves me." On the contrary, he knows that he does not deserve to be loved. And at times he writes as if everything is against him (Rom. 8:35; 1 Cor. 4:10–13; 2 Cor. 4:8–12; 2 Cor. 11:23–28). No, Paul knows that God has given His Son for him (Gal. 2:20). And if God has given His Son for him, God will stop at nothing in order to bring him to His eternal glory.

"Who can be against us?" No one, not even Satan. No opposition can withstand God's love and purposes for us.

WHO WILL BRING ANY CHARGE?

If the shield against Satan's first fiery dart is God's gift of His Son, what is our defense against the accusations that seem to match the guilt we feel?

Satan is specifically called "the accuser of our brethren" (Rev. 12:10). When he employs this dart, he accuses believers of guilt and sin, and claims these may damn them in the presence of God.

Zechariah gives us a powerful illustration of this. He sees Joshua the high priest standing before God. His clothes are filthy. The filth represents his "iniquity" (Zech. 3:4). Beside him stands Satan (v. 1), accusing him: "Look at him. Look at Joshua covered in the filth of his sin. He is not fit for the presence of God."

Satan is subtle enough to use even God's holy law to accuse us of sin. He stirs up remaining sin in our hearts, and then—once we are conscious of its presence—he begins to accuse us mercilessly.

He brings sudden temptation into our minds—perhaps distasteful, even, at times, blasphemous thoughts. Satan has much with which to accuse us. "Those things have no place in the mind of a Christian believer," he screams at us. "How can you possibly be Christ's?"

John Bunyan's masterpiece, *The Pilgrim's Progress*, gives a vivid description of this very thing: "One thing that I would not let slip. I took notice that now poor Christian was so confounded that he did not know his own voice."

What does "he did not know his own voice" mean? Bunyan explains:

And thus I perceived it [this is what he saw] just when he was come over against the mouth of the burning pit. [Here comes the fiery dart]: One of the wicked ones got behind him, and stepped up softly to him, and whisperingly suggested many grievous blasphemies to him, which he verily thought had proceeded from his own mind. This put Christian more to it than anything he met with before, even to think he should now blaspheme him that he loved so much before; yet could he have helped it, he would not have done it. But he had not the discretion neither to stop his ears nor to know from whence those blasphemies came.[25]

Blasphemies? In the mind of a Christian? Yes. Indeed, the description in Bunyan's allegory parallels his personal testimony in his autobiography, *Grace Abounding to the Chief of Sinners*. For a whole year, as he heard the gospel, his mind flooded with blasphemies.[26] Yes, blasphemies. Those are the lengths to which Satan will go.

Charles H. Spurgeon, the great nineteenth-century Baptist preacher, had a similar experience, although he had never heard anyone blaspheme Christ.

So you are not alone if you have experienced something like that. Indeed, many Christians have been oppressed by Satan in this way, and paralyzed spiritually because they have felt that no other believer could ever have experienced this. They fear they are not believers after all, and they sink into despair.

Where does this come from? It comes from the pit of hell. Bunyan's poor Pilgrim did not know at first about Satan's arts and darts. He thought it all came from himself, and that therefore he could not possibly be a Christian.

Many Christian believers who have experienced this have no idea where it comes from. They share the Pilgrim's conclusion: "I must be damned to hell if there are such blasphemies in my mind against Jesus Christ."

The Pilgrim was unable to discern the difference between the impressions that were being made on his mind by external spiritual forces and the permanent desire of the new heart that had been given to him to live for and to love Jesus Christ. But the truth was that "One of the wicked ones got behind him, and stepped up softly to him, and whisperingly suggested many grievous blasphemies to him, which he verily thought had proceeded from his own mind."[27]

Reliable Defense

What will you do if something of this order happens? Where will you go? To whom can you turn? To what will you appeal?

Can you appeal to the fact that you are a mature Christian or to the quality of your Christian service? Can you appeal to your spiritual condition and say, "I know I am usually better than that"? These are not secure defenses against this fiery dart of the Devil.

Here, as elsewhere, we can learn by sitting at the feet of the masters of the spiritual life. Martin Luther—who knew a thing or two about these attacks—emphasized the need to see that the gospel that saves us is outside us. We are not accounted righteous in God's sight either by regeneration or by sanctification. The fact that we have been born again does not justify us. It gives us a new heart, but in itself it does not provide the forgiveness of sins. No, the gospel that saves us is entirely outside us. It is Jesus Christ, incarnate, crucified for our sins, raised for our justification, who saves us.

The atonement through which we stand in a righteous, forever-justified relationship to God is neither a change in our hearts nor a new feeling. We may have all kinds of feelings as a result of justification, but justification is based on what God has done for us in Jesus.

John Newton, perhaps the wisest pastor in eighteenth-century England, well understood this harrowing experience. He wrote of being "Bowed down beneath a load of sin, by Satan sorely pressed. . . ." He then described what he did under those oppressive circumstances: "I may my fierce accuser face, and tell him . . ."

Let me pause to ask: what would you tell him? Not "I have been a better-than-average Christian" or "I made a decision for Christ twenty years ago." These are flimsy defenses against the fiery darts of the Devil. He can easily penetrate such inadequate armor.

What, then, are you to tell him? Here is Newton's counsel:

Be thou my shield and hiding place,
That sheltered near thy side,
I may my fierce accuser face
And tell him thou hast died.[28]

Satan has no weapon that can penetrate this "breastplate of righteousness." When you tell him Christ has died for you and borne God's judgment against your sin, he will be defeated. Even when he puts into your mind thoughts you hate but from which you cannot deliver yourself, his sinister accusations have no power to mar the perfection of Jesus Christ's atonement for your sin.

Your salvation rests not on what you have done but on what Christ has done. You, therefore, can be sure of it, no matter how weak the faith by which you hold on to Christ, no matter how strong the attacks and accusations of Satan may be.

Saved by Christ through Faith

Remember that you are not saved by increased levels of holiness, however desirable it is that you should reach them. Indeed, while we often say that we are "saved by faith" or by "faith in Christ," as Benjamin B. Warfield shrewdly comments, it is not even faith in Christ that saves us. It is Christ who saves us—through faith.[29] Your faith is a poor and crumbling thing, as is your spiritual service. Jesus Christ alone is qualified and able to save you because of what He has done. Cling to anything else and you are relying on flot-sam and jetsam floating on a perilous sea. It will bring you down under the waves. If you should ever experience anything like the satanic attack Bunyan's Christian endured, you will be lost. But cling to Christ Jesus and His righteousness, and nothing can sink you.

When you grasp that, you begin to realize why and how it is that you can live in the face of such demonic attacks as these. You are not pushed back on your own resources or spiritual qualities. You are able to rest exclusively on what Jesus Christ has done for you. For what He has done for you is absolutely perfect.

What Christ is doing *in you* is still incomplete. But in what Jesus Christ has done *for you* there is not a single tiny crack that the satanic arrows can penetrate. Jesus Christ is your shield. You can say, with David, "The LORD is . . . my deliverer; my God . . . in whom I will trust; my shield and the horn of my salvation, my stronghold. I will call upon the LORD, who is worthy to be praised; so shall I be saved from my enemies" (Ps. 18:2–3).

As Pastor Sibomana teaches us to sing, "My shield and buckler he."

Here is our refuge: In Christ, we are as righteous before God as Jesus Christ is righteous, for the only righteousness we have before God *is* Jesus Christ's righteousness, to which we contribute nothing.

Faith contributes nothing to that righteousness. The years we may have lived the Christian life contribute nothing to that righteousness. Conversely, our sins cannot diminish that righteousness.

Is that not a dangerous thing to say? It would be if it were distorted. But the truth is that no other kind of righteousness can justify us.

But because this is the righteousness by which we are justified, Paul can say: "Who shall bring any charge against God's elect?" (v. 33).

The answer, of course, is no one, not even—indeed, especially not—the Evil One.

WHO CAN CONDEMN US?

Satan's third fiery dart is his suggestion that despite our experience of forgiveness as Christians we still will face condemnation someday. How should we defend against this flaming arrow?

What is the difference between accusation and condemnation? Condemnation takes place when an accusation against us proves to be well-founded. As we have seen, Satan constantly accuses believers. Though he has no power to condemn them—"There is . . . no condemnation to those who are in Christ Jesus" (Rom. 8:1)—his goal is to make them *feel* condemned.

If Satan accuses me and I then respond: "You are right. I look within my heart and I see my sinfulness. I have no standing in God's presence," then Satan's condemning words will overwhelm me and I will lose my enjoyment of the grace of God.

The truth is that, in myself, I am condemned, because I remain a sinner. That is why we sometimes mistakenly listen to Satan, and we are tempted to believe him rather than to believe God. We make the mistake of listening to his accusations based on our ongoing sinfulness. We lose sight of the righteousness of Christ. Having been accused, and forgetting that our only righteousness is in Christ, we feel condemned.

This is why it is so important to rest our minds and hearts in the gospel that is outside us, on the righteousness that is in Christ that becomes ours by faith in Him.

Paul asks, "Who is he who condemns?" (v. 34a). Well, Satan certainly *seeks* to condemn. But Paul responds, "It is Christ Jesus who died, and furthermore is also risen, who is even at the right hand of God, who also makes intercession for us" (v. 34b).

Think of Simon Peter. He sinned. He denied his Lord. Isolated from Jesus and the other disciples, he must have longed for a hiding place. What fiery darts must have penetrated his conscience on that dark Jerusalem night. What self-condemning thoughts must have flooded his mind: "I didn't have the courage to stand up for my Lord, and now He is going to be crucified. There is nothing I can do about it. There's no way back for me. My situation is hopeless. I am lost."

That is a desolating experience. But sometimes true Christian believers *do* say that.

Where will you look when there is no way back for you? Paul's answer is exactly the same as Peter's: "Christ Jesus, who died, who was raised to life, is at the right hand of God, and is interceding for me."

Immediately after Peter denied his Lord a third time, Jesus turned and looked at him, and "Peter remembered the word of the Lord" (Luke 22:61). Was it *this* word: "Simon, Simon! Indeed, Satan has asked for you, that he may sift you as wheat. But I have prayed for you, that your faith should not fail; and when you have returned to Me, strengthen your brethren" (Luke 22:31–32)?

Christ's sacrifice for our sins was finished in His death on the cross. But His ministry did not cease then, or when He rose from the grave, or even when He ascended to the right hand of the Father. No, Jesus' ministry continues even now. He is present with His Father on our behalf. He is interceding for us.

What a relief it is to know this when you have made a mess of life, when you feel the accusations of Satan and condemn yourself. You are ashamed to go into the presence of God. You go to church and look around, thinking you are a hypocrite. You feel a failure—indeed, you *have* failed. Remember, then, that Jesus is at the right hand of the Father. Remember that He is there for your sake. He died for you once; He intercedes for you forever.

Before the throne of God above,
I have a strong and perfect plea.
A great High Priest whose name is Love
And ever lives and pleads for me.
My name is graven on his hands.
My name is written on his heart.
I know that while in heaven he stands,
No power can force me to depart.

When Satan tempts me to despair
And tells me of the guilt within,
Upward I look and see him there,
Who made an end of all my sin.

Because the sinless Savior died
My sinful soul is counted free,
For God the just is satisfied
To look on him and pardon me.[30]

When Satan's darts of condemnation bring you low, never forget: God never sees you as His child without first looking at you through the Son—His Son!—who is interceding for you.

WHO CAN SEPARATE US?

Satan's fourth dart prompts Paul's final question: "Who shall separate us from the love of Christ?" (v. 35). Yes, there is opposition, but it will not prevail. Yes, there is accusation, but it will not bring condemnation.

But is there still the possibility of separation?

In Paul's responses to the other questions, he is really saying, "Now, Christian, stop and let us think this through."

But here, Paul offers no argument. He has provided enough argument, logic, and debate. He does not need further arguments. He simply poses the question and responds with counter-questions that show there is only one possible answer. As he ransacks the universe for possible pressures, opposition, even catastrophe, he simply asks: "Can this, or this, or this, or this *ever* separate us from the love of God in Christ Jesus our Lord?"

Paul's answer brings us back to the beginning of the passage and points us to God's purpose for us in Christ and the absolute certainty of its fulfillment: "Whom He predestined, these He also called; whom He called, these He also justified; and whom He justified, these He also glorified" (v. 30).

God will not be frustrated in His goal of conforming us to the likeness of His Son, that He might be the Firstborn among many brothers. One day we shall stand before Him and say to Him: "Father, what was the meaning of that darkness? What was the meaning of that pressure? What was the meaning of those experiences that almost destroyed me?" His answer will be to show us—perhaps in surprising detail—that they were the instruments He was using to shape and prepare us for heaven's glory. Furthermore, we will see that everything we needed to get us through them was found in Jesus Christ.

Heraldry on Our Shield

So Paul speaks about four kinds of attack. Who is against us? Who will accuse us? Who can condemn us? Who can separate us? Against each and all of the fiery darts of the Evil One, the shield of faith in Christ—Christ Himself—is our defense.

Shields often have symbols—heraldry—emblazoned on them. What heraldry might be etched into the shield of faith?

Take a closer look. You will find in the middle a cross, and, in each of the quadrants it creates on the shield, a symbol.

In the first is the hill of Calvary, where God proved He is for us.

In the second is the justification of the ungodly, which proves that no accusation against us will stick.

In the third is the interceding Lord Jesus Christ, standing to assure us we can never be condemned.

In the fourth is the indestructible love of God that persuades us that nothing will ever be able to separate us from Jesus Christ our Lord.

When you first came in faith to Jesus Christ, you really had no idea what you were letting yourself in for, did you? Perhaps as you have gone on as a Christian believer, life has been at times almost overwhelmingly difficult for you, and so there is much in Paul's words that resonates with your experience. It is staggering to think that even before you experienced these things, the Lord had provided everything you would ever need to bring you to glory.

This is what makes grace "amazing."

If this is the world into which we have been brought, then any grace that is less than amazing will not be sufficient to see us through. But the grace of God in Jesus Christ is indeed amazing and perfectly suited to our needs. His grace will see us through.

Perhaps you stand outside all this. You may even secretly fear the thought of admitting your need of a Savior, of belonging to Christ, of turning away from sin, of letting go of the old life and coming under His Lordship.

Yet, for all you fear it, you know this is the truth. You have tried to ignore it and deny it, but you cannot any longer. There is a battle going on in your heart. Will you turn away? Or will you enter Christ's kingdom?

Stretch out your hands in faith to Jesus Christ, and He will bring you in. He will forgive you. He will keep you going. And He will take you home. Then you will fully and finally know that nothing can ever separate you from the love of God in Christ Jesus your Lord.

And you will begin to sing:

"O how the grace of God amazes me!"

6

Lord Jesus, hear my prayer,
Your grace impart;
When evil thoughts arise
Through Satan's art,
O, drive them all away
And do you, from day to day,
Keep me beneath your sway,
King of my heart.

Chapter Six

DELIVERED FROM EVIL

s there any book in the Old Testament—indeed, in the whole Bible—
that analyzes Satan's strategies in greater detail than Job?

Job experiences the full force of Satan's strategies, employed against himself and his family. Multiplied disasters strike him. Then he finds himself engaged in a series of dialogues with several friends who come to sympathize with him in his suffering but slowly begin to criticize him. They employ a simple theological formula: suffering is the specific result of sin. Job is suffering grievously. Therefore, Job must have sinned in some specific way.

Job, however, stubbornly, doggedly, refuses to accept that this is the true explanation. He will not bow to his friends' arguments.

One of these friends, Bildad, makes an eloquent speech about Job and his need; it is recorded in Job 8. Bildad says, "Behold, God will not cast away the blameless, nor will He uphold the evildoers" (Job 8:20).

Job's response is found in chapters 9 and 10. It is long, but it is worth reading slowly, for it illustrates Satan's strategies—and the defense against them—so well.

From "Darts" to "Arts"
We are tracing the marvels of God's grace by means of the themes of E. T. Sibomana's hymn, "O How the Grace of God Amazes Me."

We noted earlier that one of the more unusual features of this hymn about grace is that two of the seven verses focus on the powers of evil and the sinister darkness that Christian believers encounter in their pilgrimage. While verses three and four are devoted to the person and work of the Lord Jesus Christ, verses five and six involve reflection on the person and work of Satan.

In the previous chapter, we thought about "Satan's darts." We saw how the gospel of Jesus Christ provides us with a safeguard against "the fiery darts of the wicked one" (Eph. 6:16), by which he seeks to distort and to destroy our Christian joy.

Satan cannot ultimately destroy a Christian believer. But he is well able to destroy our assurance and our joy—our pleasure in the gospel. So we need to find in the grace of God a defense against those fiery darts of the Evil One.

But the next verse of the hymn speaks about "Satan's art": "When evil thoughts arise *through Satan's art.*"

What is "Satan's art"?

The "art" of Satan is his ability to produce sinister thoughts in the mind of the Christian believer.

By this I do not mean what the Bible regards as the works of the flesh or the lust of the eyes. Satan, of course, does work through the "eye gate" and the "passion gate" to produce evil thoughts and deceive believers, as he did in David's sin with Bathsheba. But ultimately, the most sinister thoughts that Satan insinuates into our minds are not enticements to sin but suspicions about God Himself. He always plots to cause us to "exchange the truth of God for the lie" (Rom. 1:25).

This is where the book of Job can be so helpful to us. Job's two-chapter answer to Bildad is simultaneously magnificent and terrible. In part, it speaks glorious truths about God, but it also expresses the beginning of evil thoughts about God that Satan has injected into the mind and spirit of Job.

As a sidebar, the inspiration and inerrancy of Scripture should not lead us to think that every statement in the Bible is true in an abstract sense just because it is part of God's Word. Scripture as God's inerrant Word infallibly records the lies, falsehoods, and half-truths uttered by men and women. To isolate such statements and argue that they must be true in an absolute sense because they are in the Bible would be to misunderstand Scripture and to read the Bible mistakenly, as if it were a collection of isolated axioms. In fact, it is a record of God's engagement with men and women in all of their fallen, distorted, confused, and often rebellious attitudes, thoughts, and words about Him.

Job—the Drama

The book of Job, of course, is a marvelous drama set in the ancient Near East, probably in the times of the patriarchs.

It is common to speak of "the sufferings of Job." But right from the beginning of the book we are given the explanation of those sufferings. As a result—as is often the case in Scripture—the reader knows far more about what is really happening than those who are involved ever know.

Job suffers intensely. Three friends, joined later by a fourth, the famous "Job's comforters," come to him. To their great credit, they sit with him for an entire week and say absolutely nothing. They share his loss; they are stunned into silence by the depth of his suffering.

Slowly they open a dialogue about the meaning of his suffering. That is when the sparks begin to fly.

Think of the book of Job as a drama in a theater. Before the curtain goes up, a double prologue occurs for us to watch. These scenes portray Satan, the enemy of God and therefore of man, coming into the presence of God and debating whether God can be trusted, loved, and obeyed *simply because He is God.* Satan points to earth and says to God: "You cannot be trusted, loved, and obeyed simply for Yourself. Anyone who seems to do that does it only for what he believes You will give him in return."

God replies: "Do you see My servant Job? There is a man who trusts Me, loves Me, and obeys Me. He knows Me and understands My character. You can do anything to him short of harming his person. Take from him all he has, and he will still trust Me" (see Job 1:6–12).

In a series of appalling tragedies, Satan takes almost everything from Job. He loses his possessions and most of his family. Yet Job continues to trust his God (see 1:13–22).

Satan then returns to the heavenly court and says to the Lord: "A man can lose many things, but so long as he has his health and strength he will hold on to a glimmer of hope and trust You" (see 2:4–5).

"Well, then," God replies, "I believe that My glory and honor will be sustained in this man's life. You can do anything you want to him—short of killing him—but this man will continue to trust Me" (see 2:6).

So another preliminary scene is played out before the curtain opens. Satan is allowed to have his way with Job's health—and he does:

> So Satan went out from the presence of the LORD, and struck Job with painful boils from the sole of his foot to the crown of his head. And he took for himself a potsherd with which to scrape himself while he sat in the midst of the ashes. Then his wife said to him, "Do you still hold fast your integrity? Curse God and die!" But he said to her, "You speak as one of the foolish women speaks. Shall we indeed accept good from God, and shall we not accept adversity?" In all this Job did not sin with his lips. (Job 2:7–10)

The great question that is debated in the courtroom of heaven is this: "Will Job honor God and His glory, trust Him, love Him, and serve Him because of who He is? Or will he give way?"

By contrast, all that Job's friends see is that he is suffering intensely. They do not know that Satan is jealous of God's glory and honor. Neither do they have any sense that behind the tragedies in Job's life is a life-and-death contest about God's glory and honor, and whether or not His people will trust Him absolutely.

All they can see is Job's pain. All they can do is try to help him understand why he is suffering.

So the rest of the drama follows a series of dialogues among three of these friends and Job; then a younger man, Elihu, appears and dialogues with Job; finally, God Himself steps onto the stage and addresses Job directly. Toward the end of the drama, through God's revelation of Himself, Job is found prostrated in worship before God. As the curtain finally falls, Job is delighting in the riches that God has restored to him.

Limited Understanding

The question that we, the readers of Job, are meant to ask as we reflect on these magnificent speeches is this: "Will Job discover what we already know?"

We know that he is suffering *because* God is going to glorify His honor in him. We know that he is suffering *because* he trusts in God, not because he has sinned. We know that he is suffering *because* he is the victim of the onslaught of Satan.

But all Job knows is that he is suffering. He knows no "because."

Will Job ever, at any point in these speeches and soliloquies, penetrate through the veil that clouds his understanding? Will he ever realize that he is experiencing simultaneously the most malicious activity of the Evil One to destroy his enjoyment of God and yet the sustaining grace of God to withstand an onslaught whose purpose he cannot understand? Or will he never discover it?

These are the questions.

Job 9 and 10 contain heart-rending words. Job is at the nadir of his excruciating experience. He has been oppressed rather than helped by his friends' logical argument, which is as follows:

Major Premise: All suffering is a result of sin and a judgment on it.
Minor Premise: You are suffering.
Conclusion: Therefore, you have sinned.

That is what logicians call a syllogism, a logically developed argument. Job argues to the contrary:

Major Premise: I am suffering.
Minor Premise: But I have not sinned in a specific way—as my "friends" insist.

Conclusion: Therefore, the explanation for my suffering is not my sin—although I do not know why I am suffering or what its meaning might be.

Listen to Job as we walk through what he says in chapters 9 and 10.

Job 9

In chapter 9, Job wrestles with a big question:

• In verses 1–13, he asks, in essence: "How can I possibly plead my cause before God? How can I possibly argue that I am innocent before God, because—after all—He is God. I could never argue successfully before Him."

• In verses 14–20: "Even if I did engage in argument, as in a courtroom, how could I possibly withstand the force of His questioning? God would expose me. His logic would be too powerful for me. I would not be able to stand the incessant pressure of His questioning."

• In verses 21–24: "How could *anything I say* make a difference?"

• By the end of the chapter, he goes further: "How could *anything* make any difference?"

His gut struggle is: "How can I debate this issue with God? How can I demand from Him an explanation for what I am experiencing? It seems utterly hopeless."

Nevertheless, Job says: "I would speak up without fear if I knew there was somebody to take my side in the courtroom. But as it stands, I cannot. My situation is desperate" (see 9:35).

Job 10

Yet—as is often true of us in times of personal turmoil—Job then goes on to do the very thing he said would be hopeless in the first place. Having already asked in chapter 9, "How could I possibly plead my cause before God?" he tells us what he would say to God *if he could plead his cause* before Him. So he actually ends up telling God what is on his mind (10:3–7).

The words that follow are among the most poignant in the book, if not in the whole of the Old Testament. Here is a man seeking to be faithful to

God when he cannot understand Him, and when his friends (and the enemy who stands behind them) are twisting the knife of his suffering into his soul and endangering his trust in the goodness of God.

In chapter 10, Job asks God a barrage of questions:

• Verse 3: "What are You doing to me? Why are You doing this to me? Is it for Your pleasure? Does it please You to oppress me?"

• Verse 4: "Do You see just with human eyes? Do You have eyes of flesh? Can't You see inside me to know what's happening to me?"

• Verses 5–7: "Do You have only a short time to live? Is that why You have to treat me like this—as if You were soon to die? Are Your years like those of a man, that You must search out my thoughts and probe after my sin?"

• Verses 8–12: "Why? Why, when You gave me these apparent indications of Your goodness, kindness, and love, why, why, oh why do You now hide Your real purpose from me?"

• Verses 13–17: "I see it now. This is what You concealed in Your heart. You were watching me to punish me, searching out my thoughts and probing my sin."

• Finally, in heartbreaking words recorded in verses 18–22, Job asks the God of the universe, his own Creator—as if he is no longer sure to whom he is speaking: "Why was I ever brought into the world? Why did You bring me out of the womb? It would have been better that I had gone straight from the womb to the grave. Can't You give me any respite from Your relentless attacks, so that I can have just a moment's joy before I am utterly exhausted and my life comes to an end? I wish I had never been born."

TWO CLUES

Appearances can be deceptive. But two clues help us to see what is really happening here.

The first is this: Job feels he is in total, absolute, and utter darkness. He has nowhere to go. He has no argument he can make. There seems to be no help for him in heaven or earth. Everything seems bleak. He wishes he had died in his mother's womb.

The second clue is this: The prologue to the book permits us, who are spectators, to see that Job is wrong.

As we listen to him, we can see something Job cannot yet see about himself. Yes, he is in the dark. To him, it is so dark that he cannot take in the fact that he is still able to see.

But Job can still see.

For one thing, he gives a magnificently poetic and deeply moving description of his own creation:

Your hands have made me and fashioned me,
An intricate unity;
Yet You would destroy me.
Remember, I pray, that You have made me like clay.
And will You turn me into dust again?
Did You not pour me out like milk,
And curdle me like cheese,
Clothe me with skin and flesh,
And knit me together with bones and sinews?
You have granted me life and favor,
And Your care has preserved my spirit. (Job 10:8–12)

This is struggling, agonizing faith. But it is nevertheless real faith that speaks here. It speaks eloquently of the breathtaking wonder of the Creator's handiwork. This is a profound and beautiful meditation on the gentleness, kindness, creativity, and imaginativeness of God. Job's eloquence goes far beyond what most of us could ever hope to express in describing what God has done in our creation.

So from one point of view, Job sees wonderfully.

Skewed Vision

But then look at what he also says: "But You concealed Your real purpose in Your heart." He is saying: "God, all this is just a front. All this is just a dangling carrot before the donkey. This is not Your real purpose. You have shown this kindness, but behind it, as I now realize, there has been this terrible malice" (cf. 10:13).

Psalm 102 records a similar experience: "God," the psalmist says in essence, "you lifted me up—but now you have dashed me to the ground" (Ps. 102:10b).

Is God a petulant child who opens a present on Christmas morning and, by the middle of the afternoon, has broken it and thrown it aside?

Here, then, darkness and light intermingle. Job thinks he is in blackest darkness. But listening to his words, we can tell that he is not. He sees *something*.

Most people are city dwellers and rarely if ever experience total darkness. It is impossible to do so in a modern city unless there is a power outage on a totally overcast night. There is always enough light for our eyes to adjust and to make out something in the dark.

My family used to live on the most northerly inhabited island in the United Kingdom. If the clouds came over in the middle of the night, there was no residual light. You could put your hand right up to your face and not see it. Now *that* is total darkness.

Job is *not* in that kind of darkness. The proof? He is still speaking to God.

By the grace of God, most of us never experience the kind of darkness Job did. But great darkness does overtake God's children at times. Isaiah speaks of the possibility of the children of light walking in the darkness for a season (cf. Isa. 50:10).

Imagine you are Job's pastor—or, for that matter, simply one of his friends. At this point, your task would be to persuade this man who believes he is in total darkness that he is not. You would try to take hold of these threads of light in his understanding and pull them loose in order to hold them before his eyes.

The key to helping Job would be to sit down beside him and say to him: "Job, you can actually see; your own words tell me that. You can see God. You can see grace. You can see evidences of His purpose. You see the wonder, beauty, and genius of His creating handiwork. You are not in complete darkness. You are by no means in the outer darkness."

But how could you show him this?

By asking two questions.

QUESTION ONE: WHAT IS GOD REALLY LIKE?

The question of God's nature is foundational for the Christian life. In a sense, every failure in the Christian life can be traced back to a wrong answer to this question. How we live the Christian life is always an expression of how we think about God.

"What is God really like?" is the great question of the book of Job.

Particularly poignant are Job's words in 10:13 (ESV): "Yet these things you hid in your heart; I know that this was your purpose."

They prompt us to ask, "What has God concealed in His heart?"

Job sees that God is magnificently, creatively sovereign. But he misunderstands how God uses His sovereignty: "If I called and He answered me, I would not believe that He was listening to my voice" (9:16).

What has driven Job to such perverse logic? He is suffering. He is crying out to God. But God seemingly is not listening. He appears indifferent to Job's need.

What Job does not know is that Satan is the immediate instrument and agent of his suffering. There is a confusion of identities in his mind. It is Satan who will not give Job relief or peace.

That is exactly "Satan's art." He seeks to distort our view of God and our understanding of His gracious character. The result is that our disposition toward God becomes twisted. We begin to think about God, and respond to Him, *as though He had the identity of the Evil One.* Satan's plan is to blind us to God's grace and to diminish our trust in Him, crushing our love for Him and destroying all the pleasures of grace.

Listen again to Job: "You have made me like clay" (10:9). But now he believes God is watching him: "If my head is exalted, you hunt me like a fierce lion. . . . You renew your witnesses against me" (10:16–17).

Do you see how different that is from the first chapters of Job? God said: "This man trusts Me. This man loves Me. I can stake My reputation on this man." God is not against Job; rather, He is confident in the work He has done within him. Job is, as it were, God's best pupil—he trusts God simply because He is God and has shown Himself to be totally trustworthy.

It is this trust that Satan is seeking to destroy.

Satan does this by a damnable strategy. He seeks to confuse Job about the real identity of his assailant. Once Satan has had some success, Job begins to say things about God that are demonstrably false. He is on the verge of "exchanging the truth of God for the lie" (Rom. 1:25).

Thus, as John Calvin says, "Satan's aim is to drive the saint to madness by despair."[31]

It is a terrible thing to see Christians driven to the brink of despair because of this confusion of identities between God and Satan. The fierce warrior who attacks them (as Job 16:14 describes him) is not the God and Father of our Lord Jesus Christ. It is His enemy, the Evil One. Thankfully, as Martin Luther used to say, "the Devil is God's devil"—God has not abdicated His throne.

Flashes of Light

Notice that there are small flashes of light here.

Look at the wording of Job 10:16: "If my head is exalted, You hunt me like a fierce lion."

Of what does that remind you? Surely of 1 Peter 5:8–9: "Be sober, be vigilant; because your adversary the devil walks about like a roaring lion, seeking whom he may devour. Resist him, steadfast in the faith. . . ."

If we were spectators at "Job—The Drama" in a theater, we would want to throw a New Testament onto the stage and shout: "Job, you are right to think you are being devoured by a lion—but read 1 Peter 5:8–9. It contains the clue." The way Job is describing God here is the way the New Testament describes Satan. There has been a confusion of identities, engineered by the Deceiver. No wonder Job is near despair.

Later, Job again expresses this same sense of mistaken identity: "I was at ease, but He has shattered me; He also has taken me by the neck, and shaken me to pieces; He has set me up for His target, His archers surround me. He pierces my heart and does not pity; He pours out my gall on the ground" (Job 16:12–13).

Again, think of yourself as a spectator, watching this drama unfold, hearing this language pour from the depths of Job's soul. What do you instinctively want to do? Again, you want to pick up a New Testament, throw it onto the stage, and shout: "Job, read Ephesians 6:10–18. You are not wrestling against flesh and blood here. God has provided armor for you to wear."

Poor Job is like a man groping for a clue to an experience that mystifies him.

For a moment, it seems the truth is almost within his grasp. The one who confronts him is like a lion seeking to devour him and at the same time an enemy who is firing darts at him to destroy him. Can this really be God? Would He be so merciless in His assaults?

In his response to Bildad (Job 9), Job cries out in words that leap off the page. They stand out like a beacon of light in the midst of the darkness. He is describing what he thinks God is doing to him. But then there is a momentary flash of light. He wonders whether perhaps things are not as they appear to be. Can there be another, very different explanation for all he is going through? He cries out: "If it is not He, *who else could it be*?" (v. 24, emphasis added).

At this point more than any other, if you were a spectator of this drama, you would surely want to shout as loudly as possible: "Job, it isn't God who is doing this. He loves you. He has staked His reputation on your safekeeping. Satan is the one who is doing all this to you, Job. You're almost there. Oh, Job, keep asking your question: 'If it isn't You, God, who else can it be?' Perhaps you will break through to the answer."

But Satan continues to wear him down, not least through his friends.

Although their speeches contain some of the most sublime theology to be found anywhere in the Bible, their false application of the truth is threatening to destroy Job. It certainly can never save him or bring him into the light.

As Satan deceives him, and then wears him down, it is as if he is saying: "Job, I have you in my grasp now. I have you! You are beginning to confuse my character with God's. That is exactly my plan. I mean to bring you to the point where you will hate Him."

A Well-Tested Strategy

At the very beginning of the Bible, Satan successfully employed the same strategy against Eve. In the guise of a serpent, Satan said: "Don't you see that God has put you in this wonderful garden but conceals His malignant disposition toward you? Didn't He say, 'You are not to eat the fruit of any of these trees'?"

God had actually said: "All this is yours. I give it to you to express My love for you and My joy in you. But I want you to show Me that you trust Me and love Me in return. I want to have the kind of relationship with you in which you are content to be man rather than God. I want you to obey me, not simply because of what I have given you, but because you trust Me as a good and gracious God. So I command you not to eat the fruit of one particular tree—the tree of the knowledge of good and evil. At the moment, I will not fully explain why I am giving you this command. I simply want you to trust Me. I want you to be confirmed in your love and obedience to Me. I want you to show that you really do believe I am a gracious God and that I can be trusted in everything."

But Satan whispered to Eve: "Has God forbidden *every fruit* in the garden?" Eve attempted to discuss the issue. But within a few minutes, she was—by her own admission—deceived (Gen. 3:13). In fact, God had given every single fruit to the man and woman for their pleasure—except one. Only the tree of the knowledge of good and evil was off limits.

Why? Was this tree poisonous? Probably not. It is described in the same terms as all the other fruit trees (cf. Gen. 3:6 with Gen. 2:9). But God had appointed this specific tree as the test case. Love for Him and trust in Him could grow only under test conditions. This was the test: God was saying: "Do as I ask you, simply because you know I am the One who is asking you. Show you love Me by putting My will first. In that way you will grow in your understanding of what is good."

But Eve listened to the wrong voice. Perhaps, after all, God was withholding something good from them. "Doesn't that fruit look good?" insinuated the Serpent. "Why would God deny you something good?" Eve took the fruit. Adam followed. The rest, as the saying goes, is history.

Eve was deceived into believing what Satan said about God rather than what God revealed about Himself.

Adam and Eve exchanged the truth about God for a lie.

This is the ultimate explanation for the deep-seated and only thinly disguised fear in unbelievers' hearts that God means to do them more harm than good. After all, if you really believed that the all-kind Creator of the universe wanted to bless and enrich your life, would you not seek Him?

For all their protestations that they believe in a God of love, deep down people believe the opposite. They fear that God is out to destroy their lives. They do not trust Him; they do not love Him; they do not obey Him; they do not worship Him; they do not want Him. They too have exchanged the truth about God for the lie.

But even believers who have made some progress in their pilgrimage find themselves confronted by the same lie. It can force itself on us because of circumstances, trials, and perplexities. It comes through "Satan's art." Why would he retire a weapon he has so successfully used throughout the millennia?

If you know that God is your loving Father and believe that He is generous in lavishing His kindness on you; if you know that He will keep you in this world until your work is done, that you will lack no good thing, and that at the end of your life He will take you into His presence forever—all because He loves you—should you not trust Him in every situation?

Satan hates to see us tasting the life-transforming blessings of enjoying God. Perhaps it is because he has forfeited them himself. That is why he engages in this deception of identity confusion. This is why he does everything in his power to twist our thoughts of God.

He whispers: "Perhaps God is concealing something from you. Perhaps His Word is not true. Perhaps He wants to spoil your life. Have you considered that?"

If we listen to such words, it should not surprise us that a confusion of identities begins to take place in our minds. Soon we may impute to God some of the characteristics of His archenemy, the Devil. This is, paradoxically, exactly what Satan wants.

The Christian, therefore, shares in Job's conflict, even if he or she does not share his terrible sufferings.

The Lord is absolutely good, true, faithful, and gracious. But the enjoyment of Him is in large measure dependent on what we think He is really like.

That is why deceiving us about the character of God is central to Satan's strategy against us.

QUESTION TWO: WHERE CAN I FIND HELP?

If the first question is, "What is God really like?" the second question Job must ask is, "Where can I find help?"

Job makes another significant statement about God: "He is not a man, as I am, that I may answer Him, and that we should go to court together. Nor is there any mediator between us, who may lay his hand on us both" (9:32–33).

He says: "If only there were someone to arbitrate between us—someone who was powerful like God and yet understood what it means to be weak and human like me. If only there were a person who could place one of his hands on almighty God and the other on me. Then, somehow, he might hold on to both of us and bring us together. If only there were someone like that to arbitrate, then, perhaps . . ."

Later, he goes even further: "O earth, do not cover my blood, and let my cry have no resting place! Surely even now my witness is in heaven, and my evidence is on high. My friends scorn me; my eyes pour out tears to God. Oh, that one might plead for a man with God, as a man pleads for his neighbor" (Job 16:18–21).

Job is like a man who has gone into a dark room. He stumbles and reaches out to grab someone's arm for security. But he cannot see the person he is holding. He has gripped the arm of someone who has been in the room all the time. But who is it? Is there, after all, a Friend in heaven to take up his case?

As Job stumbles in the dark, he utters the most heartrending cry of the whole drama. We, the spectators, realize it:

"If it is not He, who else could it be?" (Job 9:24b).

Here Job almost touches the light switch in his darkened room. The sinister hand at work in his life is almost revealed—a supernatural hand, but not the hand of God. If only he could flick the switch he would see his enemy. If only he had a Mediator, he could be at peace.

This is exactly what we all need. Brave Job has stumbled on the most important clue to anchor his soul in the midst of the storm. His darkness is a result of Satan's art—his attack on Job's desire to glorify God in everything. Satan will even distort the character of God in his eyes in order to destroy his trust in and love for the great and glorious Creator. But Job holds on to a glimmer of hope that someone—Someone, as we know, like the Lord Jesus Christ—might come to his rescue.

According to the apostle John, the Son of God came into the world in order to destroy the works of the Devil (1 John 3:8). Only the God-Man could place one hand on God and the other on man, and say, "Now we will be together." In order to be our Savior, He took our flesh; He became a member of our family, experienced our suffering, and tasted the outer darkness, crying out on the cross of Calvary, "My God, My God, why have You forsaken Me?" (Matt. 27:46). He entered Job's darkness, fought against Job's enemy, and trusted Job's God in impenetrable blackness. He has detailed qualifications to be our Savior.

The Only Answer

So Job hangs on as he wrestles with the two questions that confront him: "What is God really like?" and "Where can I find help?"

The answer to both questions is one and the same.

But what?

When we are in the darkness, there is no point in pretending to be in the light, is there? We cannot point to things in our lives and say: "Well, that's going well. So maybe it's not as bad as I thought." No, when we are in the darkness, that answer provides no comfort.

"Well," we might say, "see the blessings I once enjoyed." But those blessings of the past may seem like the blessings of Job's past. "Yes," he said, "I see these blessings. But was God concealing a different and more sinister purpose behind them?"

There is ultimately only one place we can go to answer these questions: "God demonstrates His own love toward us, in that while we were still sinners, *Christ died for us*" (Rom. 5:8, emphasis added).

You cannot rely on your experiences to prove the love of God. They may indeed give you evidences of it. But when you are in the dark, those very things may seem to mock you.

There is one place you can go. The Scottish theologian James Denney once said that the only thing in which he ever envied a Roman Catholic priest was in his ability to hold out a crucifix before a congregation and say, "God loves you like that."

We do not need that symbol to proclaim the reality to ourselves. For, as Paul argues in Romans 8:32, God did not spare His own Son but gave Him up to the cross for us all. There is no other evidence or argument that can be brought in all the dark providences of human experience that can withstand the mighty logic of the evidence of Calvary. If God has said, "I love you so much that I gave My Son in your place," you can trust Him in everything and for everything.

> *I need no other argument,*
> *I need no other plea,*
> *It is enough that Jesus died,*
> *And that He died for me.*[32]

All of us at times find ourselves faced with these two great questions. They are far from trivial. They are the most important questions in the world: "What is God really like?" and "Where can I find help?"

The answer to both questions is found in a single word: Jesus.

If you are in the dark, whether inside the kingdom of Christ or outside the kingdom of Christ, this is where you need to go first: to Jesus the Savior, who died for us on the cross.

Trust in Him. He foils Satan's arts.

7

Come now, the whole of me,
Eyes, ears, and voice.
Join me, creation all,
With joyful noise:
Praise him who broke the chain
Holding me in sin's domain
And set me free again!
Sing and rejoice!

Chapter Seven

TRUE FREEDOM

We began our exploration of God's grace by noting that many Christian hymns speak about it as "surprising" or "amazing." Yet we often do not seem very amazed by grace.

It is, sadly, possible to be un-amazed by the grace of God, to take it for granted, as though it were ours by right or, worse, by merit. Thus, we *dis*-grace the grace of God. In the process, the melody line of the Christian life is lost.

E. T. Sibomana's hymn, "O How the Grace of God Amazes Me," shows us how to be amazed by grace all over again. Its final verse returns to the theme with which it began. Why is grace so amazing? It is because grace sets us free.

But we return to this theme at a different level. We are encouraged to:

Praise him who broke the chain
Holding me in sin's domain
And set me free again!
Sing and rejoice!

Paul develops this theme at length in Romans 6. It is one of the most important chapters in the New Testament. A working knowledge of it is essential.

The letter to the Romans was written to Christians who—in the main—had never met Paul. In it, he explains what he calls "my gospel" (Rom. 2:16; 16:25). He assumes they should be familiar with many of the things he wants to say to them. In chapter 6, he appeals to the significance of their baptism to help them grasp the fact that they have died to the old life and been raised into a new one. He points out that we are "free from sin" (6:18).

Paul sees this teaching as fundamental to the Christian life.

Sometimes we imagine that our greatest need is to move on to the "higher" or "deeper" teaching of the gospel. But in fact, our real need is to get a deeper and firmer grasp of the main truths of the gospel. Weakness here tends to lead to weakness everywhere. Paul sees that we need to think long and hard about what it means to be a Christian, and especially about what it means to be united to Christ. That is certainly true in Romans 6. Its teaching is as fundamental to the Christian life as it is stretching to the Christian's mind.

Paul asks a basic question: "Do you really understand how the grace of God works?"

Free from Sin's Dominion, Living in its Presence

It may help us to get our bearings if we put his teaching in summary form before we look at the details:

- The Christian has *already* been delivered from the *reign* of sin.
- But the Christian is *not yet* set free from the *presence* of sin.
- Therefore, the Christian must *resist* sin, for he is no longer its servant.

The dominion, or reign, of sin has been broken through our union with Christ. In Christ, we are no longer the people we once were; we belong to the new creation—the old has passed away, the new has come (2 Cor. 5:17).

We have died to sin; we can no longer live in it.

This is such an important principle that the greatest of the Puritan theologians, John Owen, saw it as fundamental to all pastoral counseling:

Wherefore, there are two things hard and difficult in this case:

1. To convince those in whom sin evidently hath the dominion that such indeed is their state and condition. . . .

2. To satisfy some that sin hath not the dominion over them, notwithstanding its restless acting itself in them and warring against their souls; yet unless this can be done, it is impossible they should enjoy peace and comfort in this life.[33]

In Adam and in Christ

Paul's words in Romans 6:1–14 do not simply drop out of the sky. They are integrally related to his argument in the preceding section of Romans 5:12–21. There, Paul describes the effects of Adam's sin and how they impact the whole of humanity.

Adam was the first man. In that capacity, he was also the representative of the whole human race before God. His fall carried implications for the whole of humanity. In that sense, we all share in Adam's sin. We all sinned and we all die in Adam (Rom. 5:12–14).

But there is good news in the gospel. God has sent a second Adam, Jesus Christ (strictly speaking, "the last Adam"; 1 Cor. 15:45). He also represents all of His people in undoing what Adam did and in doing what he failed to do.

O loving wisdom of our God!
When all was sin and shame,
A second Adam to the fight
And to the rescue came.

O wisest love! that flesh and blood,
Which did in Adam fail,
Should strive afresh against the foe,
Should strive and should prevail.[34]

So, Paul argues, just as the disobedience of the one man Adam constituted many as sinners, so through the obedience of Christ, the new Adam, many will be constituted righteous. As a result, where sin abounded in the world, grace has now super-abounded (Rom. 5:20b).

As Isaac Watts put it:

In Him the tribes of Adam boast
More blessings than their father lost.[35]

Paul realized that someone might well respond to this teaching by saying: "What you are saying—that more sin has led to more grace—implies that the more we sin, the more God is going to manifest His grace. If that is the case, the logic of your teaching is that we can sin to our hearts' content so that grace may abound."

Is that the logical implication of Paul's teaching? "Shall we continue in sin that grace may abound?" (Rom. 6:1). On the contrary, Paul responds, the logic of grace is the exact opposite: rather than *"more sin leads to more grace*, so we may go on sinning," the truth is that *"more grace leads to less sin*, because grace delivers us from sin."

This truth becomes the platform on which Paul builds his teaching in Romans 6. Becoming a Christian involves nothing less than a radical deliverance from the dominion of sin.

How does Paul prove this? One helpful way to plot our course through his answer is by asking four basic questions about his teaching.

QUESTION ONE—WHY?

Question: Why does the Christian no longer continue in sin?
Answer: Because the Christian died to sin and therefore cannot go on living in it.

Paul responds on two levels to the suggestion that we continue in sin so that grace will abound. First, he gives a "gut reaction." He responds at the level of Christian instinct. Then he provides a theological response at the level of Christian understanding and reasoning.

The growing Christian responds to everything in this twofold way. On the one hand, we develop Christian instincts as a sportsman develops "muscle memory." Biblically informed reactions become "second nature" to us. But we also develop a Christian mind that understands the motivations that drive godly instincts and the connection between gospel truth and gospel life.

Paul's initial response to the question is, "Certainly not!" (Rom. 6:2a), or more vividly in the King James Version, "God forbid!" "Shall we continue in sin that grace may abound?" "No!" he says, "God forbid!"

That is an instinctive response. Paul does not need to stop, look up verses in his Bible, then think the issue through. He instinctively knows that such a question must be based on a false premise. Anything that is contrary to the holy character of God and a holy lifestyle clearly cannot be consistent with the gospel.

But Paul also carefully responds at the level of the Christian mind. He follows his own principle, "Be infants in evil, but in your thinking be mature" (1 Cor. 14:20, ESV). This is why his explanation begins with his characteristic "Do you not *know* . . . ?" (Rom. 6:3, emphasis added). The transformation of our lives takes place through the renewal of our minds: right thinking about the truth of the gospel motivates right living in the power of the gospel (Rom. 12:1–2).

The Logic of Grace

Why, then, does greater grace not justify greater sin? Simple—the nature and the logic of grace forbid it: "How shall we who died to sin live any longer in it? Do you not know that as many of us as were baptized into Christ Jesus were baptized into His death?" (Rom. 6:2b–3).

Baptism is a naming ceremony. We are baptized into the name of Christ (Matt. 28:18–20). We are transferred symbolically from one family connection into another, from the family of Adam into the family of Jesus Christ. We no longer have the identity we once did.

Baptism also points to how this transfer takes place—by our union with Christ in his death to sin and his resurrection into new life. The implications are profound: If we have died to sin and been raised into new life in Christ, it follows that we no longer can live to the sin to which we have died.

What is the logic here?

• Christ Jesus *died and was raised.*

• Christ's death was *a death He died to sin* and His resurrection was *a resurrection into newness of life* (Rom. 6:10).

• We were baptized *into* Christ Jesus.

• In being baptized *into* Christ, we were baptized into *His death to sin and His resurrection into newness of life.*

Therefore:

• By being baptized into union with Christ, we have been baptized *into His death to sin and His life to God.*

• Since this is so, we—having been baptized into Him in His death to sin and raised into His new life—can no longer live to sin.

Paul's words are actually very carefully nuanced. His words "*How shall we who died to sin* live any longer in it?" (v. 2, emphasis added) might be better translated along these lines: "*We who are the kind of people who died to sin*, how can such as we live in it any longer?" To live in sin would be a contradiction of the kind of people we have become in Christ.

So the answer to question one, "Why does the Christian no longer continue in sin?" is that the Christian is no longer the person he or she once was, and therefore no longer lives out the former lifestyle. Having died to sin, we cannot go on living in it.

But this raises a second question.

QUESTION TWO—WHAT?

Question: What does it mean to have died to sin?
Answer: We are set free from sin's reign and are no longer under its authority.

Every Christian has died to sin. If you have not died to sin, you are not a Christian. It is as starkly simple as that.

The expression "died to sin" occurs only here in the New Testament. What does it mean?

Notice what Paul does *not* mean.

First, Paul is not using the present tense. He is not saying that we *are dying* to sin. He is not talking about something that *is happening* but something that *has happened.*

Second, Paul is not using the imperative mood (the "command mode" of a verb). He is not saying, "You *must die* to sin." He is not even saying, "*Go on dying* to sin." He is saying that we *have died.* He is not speaking of something that we accomplish, but of something that is already true of us.

Third, Paul is not saying that we have become immune to sin. That view has sometimes been popular. It is expressed in J. B. Phillips' paraphrase: "A dead man can safely be said to be immune to the power of sin."[36]

I once met a Christian who claimed to be sin-free. In the course of our discussion, she became very irritated, argumentative, and then angry. But she did not seem to regard that as sin.

Paul is clearly not saying the Christian is immune. That is contrary to the teaching of the rest of the New Testament in general, to personal experience, and to what Paul says later in this chapter when he urges us to resist sin (Rom. 6:11–14)—an exhortation that would be unnecessary if we were immune to it.

What, then, is this death to sin?

The broader context helps us here. Throughout Romans 5:12–6:23, Paul virtually personifies sin—that is, he uses personal language to describe sin's nature and influence. Sin, he says, is not an isolated act of disobedience but a power that grips and controls us. Thus, sin is a king who reigns (5:21; 6:12), a slave-owner whose servants we are (6:6, 16), and a general whose weapons we have become (6:13—"instruments"; the Greek word is *hopla*, "weapons"). He also speaks of "the wages of sin" (6:23)—sin is an employer whose salary structure for sinners brings them only death.

So from Romans 5:12 to Romans 6:23 (and beyond), Paul thinks of sin chiefly as a sinister power that enslaves us. We are mastered by it, addicted to it—as battered wives sometimes are to their vicious husbands—and powerless to set ourselves free from it.

What difference does being "in Christ" make?

This: formerly, sin was our king, owner, general, and employer. But no longer. We have been set free. In Christ's death to sin's dominion, we have died with Him. Thus, sin has no further claims on us. We are no longer its citizens, no longer under its rule or authority, although we continue to feel its influence.

We have left one kingdom and have become citizens of another. We now belong to the community of those who have died to the kingdom of sin. Sin no longer reigns over us as our king.

Paul makes this same point succinctly in Colossians 1:13–14: "Through Jesus Christ we have been delivered from the kingdom of sin and darkness and translated into the kingdom of grace and light."

Imagine that you have taken citizenship in another country from the land of your birth. Your former king or president demands your loyalty. You are entitled to respond, "You no longer have authority over me." In fact, it would be contradictory for us as citizens of our new country to live as if we were under the authority of the old one. Similarly, to go on living in sin when we have died to it is a kind of betrayal of our true identity in Christ.

The Need for Clarity

You may have been a Christian for some time and yet not grasped your new status in Christ. You may still be intimidated by the domineering character of the tyrant who once ruled over you.

Believers sometimes wrongly assume: "I have sinned; therefore, sin still has authority over me. I cannot possibly have 'died' to sin."

Paul unambiguously contradicts this thinking. Sin has no authority over anyone who is in Christ. You are no longer under its dominion. You have received a new identity. You have died out of that old kingdom. You have been raised through Christ into the new kingdom where He—not sin—reigns. From this vantage point, you can look back to your former king and his kingdom, and say: "You once ruled over me, but no longer. I am a citizen of the kingdom of my Lord and Savior, Jesus Christ. He alone reigns over me now." You may not yet be what one day you shall be; but thank God you are no longer what you once were (Rom. 6:17–18).

Paul asks the Roman Christians: "Don't you know this? Was there a slip-up in the teaching you were given? Around the time you were baptized and came into the fellowship of Jesus Christ, did no one tell you that this is what it means to be a Christian?"

Perhaps that was true in some of the early churches. Believers did not always know these things. Perhaps no one told them. If so, it is all the more likely to be true in contemporary churches. Perhaps no one has explained to you that no matter what Tyrant Sin, in all his various guises, may say, we are no longer under his dominion. He no longer has grounds for blackmail. He has no right to paralyze us into thinking that we can never make any real advance in the Christian life because we will never be free from this prevailing sin.

I enjoy reading crime novels and have frequently relaxed on long journeys by reading the novels of Anne Perry. Many of them are set in nineteenth-century London.

One of her central characters is a detective named William Monk (not to be confused with the American TV detective Adrian Monk). His life and adventures are made the more intriguing by an event in his past. While a police officer in London, he was thrown from a horse-drawn cab driven at high speed. Monk survived but lost his memory. As a result, he finds himself in situations where he is at a great disadvantage because he has no memory of what happened to him in the past. He does not know who he really was, so he does not clearly understand who he really is.

That is a basic problem for many Christians. We lose touch with the person Scripture says we really are. Perhaps we never really understood that becoming a Christian meant receiving a new identity in Christ.

Paul is saying: "Christians of Rome, you need to understand who you really are. You are people with a new citizenship. You are no longer under the dominion of sin. That makes a radical difference to the way you live the Christian life. It releases you from captivity."

It is easy to read this passage, and say: "Paul, you are not talking about me. I certainly don't think of myself as someone who has died to sin."

If that is true, a serious accident has taken place. You are like William

Monk, constantly in situations you cannot handle properly because you suffer from spiritual amnesia. You do not clearly understand your identity in Christ. You are always trying to piece things together, but never getting the picture clearly.

But when you begin to understand that in Christ you died to sin and have now been delivered from the dominion of sin; that you are no longer under its bondage; that you no longer need to be a victim of its subtle paralysis—then you find yourself saying not only "Isn't this amazing grace?" but "What glorious freedom Jesus Christ has bought for me on the cross."

QUESTION THREE—HOW?

Question: How have we died to sin?
Answer: We have died to sin through being united to Jesus Christ in faith so that we have also come to share in His death to sin and His resurrection to new life.

What have we learned?

First, Christians cannot continue in sin because we have died to sin.

Second, dying to sin means that we are delivered from sin's reign and are no longer under its authority (even though we have not yet been delivered from sin's presence).

This third question, therefore, is absolutely critical: *How have we died to sin?*

Paul answers, "Think about what baptism means." Don't you know that all who have been baptized were baptized *into* Christ Jesus? That means we were baptized into His death and His resurrection.

Baptism—Paul is speaking of water baptism—is a visible sign of all that we receive by faith in Jesus Christ.

Viewed simply as something done with water, baptism is nothing of itself. The water is just ordinary water. But as a sign with its own meaning, baptism becomes a mirror of the spiritual riches we have in Christ. The faith that responds to the sign of baptism takes hold of Jesus Christ and unites us to Him in such a way that everything that He has done for us actually becomes ours the moment we believe.

Christ died *for* our sins, but He also died *to* sin, that is, to sin's dominion. He has been raised into new resurrection life. Thus, the moment I believe in (to) Jesus Christ, I share in His death to the dominion of sin and am united to Him in the power of His resurrection into newness of life—the new life that He lives forever to God (Rom. 6:10).

In this way, the old powers that held me in their grip have been decisively overthrown. The old citizenship that kept me a prisoner to sin is annulled once and for all.

Notice how Paul explains this in Romans 6:5: "For if we have been united together in the likeness of His death, certainly we also shall be in the likeness of His resurrection."

"Certainly we also shall be . . ." Do you know this?

This perspective is not based on our feelings. We learn it from God's Word. If you do not know this, you must devote yourself to learning it. Study this passage and others like it (e.g., Col. 3:1–16). Keep asking the Lord to help you to understand His Word and to let it dwell in you richly. Chew on these passages like a dog gnaws a bone. Persevere with this teaching until it grips you. Struggle with it until it dawns on you, and you say: "O how the grace of God amazes me!"

The Old Man Crucified

The heart of Paul's teaching lies in the tightly wound statement he makes in Romans 6:6–7: ". . . knowing this, that our old man was crucified with Him, that the body of sin might be done away with, that we should no longer be slaves of sin. For he who has died has been freed from sin."

What does he mean?

First, since becoming a Christian means being united to Jesus Christ, "our old man [literally, "old" or "former" man] was crucified with Him." What does Paul mean?

Romans 6:1–14 is built on Romans 5:12–21. There Paul places the universality of sin and the wonder of salvation in their most basic context. His teaching can be expressed in simple terms:

By nature we are in Adam. Adam was the first man, but he was also the father and representative head of the whole human race. As such, his response to God's command determined the status of the whole human family.

Adam sinned and fell. In him we also sinned. In addition, since we share in his humanity, his sin spread to us all. The result is that in Adam all have sinned and all die. Our union with Adam brings us under sin's guilt and power; in Adam, we are dominated by the old order.

But God has begun again in Jesus Christ—He is the new Adam.

By grace we are in Christ. Like Adam, Christ was our representative head. He came as the second Adam.

Unlike Adam, Jesus was obedient. The New Man reversed the disobedience of the first man. The effect of Jesus' obedience in life and in death is the opposite of the effect of Adam's disobedience. His obedience brings justification instead of condemnation, and life instead of death.

So Paul's teaching in Romans 5:12–21 can be summarized in this way:

• Two men, Adam and Christ, were appointed by God as representative heads.

• Two opposite responses to God marked their lives: Adam disobeyed, Jesus obeyed.

• Two results followed: death in the case of Adam, life in the case of Christ. The old, fallen order was established in Adam; the new order is established in Christ.

By nature, then, we belong to Adam's family and are under the dominion of sin; we live within the sphere of rebellion against God. But now that we have come to Christ, we have been transferred from the family of that old man, Adam, into the family of the second Adam, the New Man, Jesus Christ.

The result of all this is that "the old man"—all that we were when united to Adam—has died.

Our biographies as Christians are written in two volumes: "Volume 1" describes our former life without Christ; "Volume 2" describes our new life in Christ. But Paul means more than this. These are two kingdoms, two families, two orders of reality to which men and women belong, by nature and by grace, in Adam and in Christ.

So becoming a Christian is not simply like learning a foreign language. We actually have become citizens of a new kingdom, members of a new family. The grip of the old order on us has been broken. The connection with Adam has been snapped. The influences that dominated our lives have been overcome. The "spell" of sin over us has been broken once and for all. Yes, indeed, "our old man was crucified."

But how can the reign of sin have been broken when we continue to sin and experience an ongoing conflict with the flesh?

Think of it this way. A man has been delivered from an addiction. Does he instantaneously become a perfect physical specimen? No; he may have caused great damage to himself. Is he now free from temptation? Not at all. Yet the reign of his addiction over him has been broken. He is now free to begin again, to undo what was badly done, and to grow into physical, moral, and spiritual health.

When a person is delivered from an addiction, the effects remain and the "pull" of the old life lingers on. Constant vigilance is essential. It is exactly the same with "addiction" to sin (and we are all by nature addicts to sin in one form or another). The addiction is broken so that its energy no longer dominates our lives. We no longer want it; it is not part of the family life we now enjoy. But while we no longer want the old way, we are not finally delivered from its ongoing influence. Increasingly sanctified we may be, but we are not yet glorified. We are free from sin's cruel dominion, but we are not yet free from its seductive presence. So we battle against its influence for the rest of our lives.

But being *influenced by* indwelling sin is not the same as being *under its dominion*. In Christ, grace reigns. We are free. We are under a new authority.

The Body of Sin Nullified

Paul now says that the old man "was crucified with Him [Christ], *that the body of sin might be done away with,* that we should no longer be slaves of sin" (Rom. 6:6, emphasis added). By "the body of sin" Paul probably means the physical human body.

The Bible does not teach that the body as such is sinful. But our bodies have become the instruments of sin and they share in our addiction to it.

In and through our bodies, sin reigns. It expresses that reign through the eyes, the ears, the hands, the tongue, the feet. The body, by nature, is dominated by sin. "But," says Paul, "in this body—yes, *this* body—I have been delivered from the dominion of sin. The old man has been crucified with Christ in order that this body, *as a body in which sin once reigned*, might no longer be the body in which sin *now* reigns."

When a fever threatens our health, we are held in its grip. But then the fever breaks and the body is able to recover. It is the same body; it may continue to bear the marks of having been fever-ridden. But it is now healthy. Slowly it begins to grow in strength.

This is how it is in the Christian's life. Our ultimate addiction to the dominion of sin is broken. Yes, the body will be set free from the presence of sin and made perfect only in the resurrection. But the body in which the Christian lives is now, by grace, infertile soil for sin and fertile soil for holiness. But "infertile" soil is not "impossible" soil. This is why Paul urges us to continue to show the greatest vigilance (Rom. 6:11–14).

The Christian Sanctified

Paul later says in Romans 12:1–2 that holiness comes to expression through the very same instrument sin used to express itself: "I appeal to you therefore, brothers, by the mercies of God, to present your bodies as a living sacrifice, holy and acceptable to God, which is your spiritual worship. Do not be conformed to this world, but be transformed by the renewal of your mind. . . ."

A transformed life is expressed in your body: through your eyes and what you see; through your ears and what you hear; through your hands and what you touch; through your tongue and what you say; and through your feet and where you go. All is to become fertile soil for Christ. So we sing: "Take my life and let it be consecrated, Lord, to thee. . . . Take my hands . . . my feet . . .

my voice . . . my lips . . . my will . . . my heart . . . myself."[37] In other words, "Take all I am in the body; all is Yours now, Lord Jesus."

All this depends on "the renewal of your mind." In other words, "Think!" That is what we need to learn to do.

Think of it especially if you have given your body over to sin. Jesus Christ can recover that body through His grace and for His glory. He can transform you, because in Him you are set free from the dominion of sin. That is exactly what Paul is saying: "our old man [self] was crucified with Him [Christ], *that the body of sin might be done away with [rendered fruitless], that we should no longer be slaves of sin*" (emphasis added).

Some who are Christ's nevertheless feel they are still slaves to sin. They do not usually share that secret with anyone. They have struggled with strong temptations to particular sins and have fallen back into believing they remain slaves to sin.

Be crystal clear about this: Christians are slaves to Jesus Christ, not to sin. We have been set free from slavery to sin. But it is possible to be deluded by the presence of sin in our lives into thinking that we are still under its dominion.

Every so often during the second half of the twentieth century, news would come of the discovery of a soldier living in the jungle years after the end of the war in which he had fought. The war was over; these men had long been free; they could have lived out in society without fear of capture, without terror of the enemy. But they did not know the truth about their situation and status.

So it is sometimes with Christians. We can be deluded by the ongoing presence of sin into thinking that we are slaves of sin. We may even be driven to despair. We fail to appreciate that the grace of God in Jesus Christ sets us free from sin's dominion and therefore enables us to engage in open conflict with sin's presence and overcome it.

So here is the answer to the question, "How have we died to sin?" We have been united to Jesus Christ in His death to sin and His resurrection to new life. We have been raised into a new order of reality altogether—where sin no longer reigns because grace reigns.

QUESTION FOUR—WHAT?

Question: What are the implications of this teaching?
Answer: We are called first to believe this teaching and then to live in the light of it.

Question one was: "Why does the Christian no longer continue in sin?"

The answer: The Christian died to sin and therefore cannot go on living in it.

Question two was: "What does it mean to have died to sin?"

The answer: We are delivered from sin's reign and are no longer under its authority.

Question three was: "How have we died to sin?"

The answer: We have died to sin in that we are united to Jesus Christ in faith and share in His death to sin and resurrection to new life.

Paul answers the fourth question to teach us the practical outworking of the gospel.

First, he says, "Likewise you also, reckon yourselves to be dead indeed to sin, but alive to God in Christ Jesus our Lord" (Rom. 6:11). Do not misunderstand Paul. He is not saying that we will die to sin *only if we believe we have died to sin.* He is saying that, if you are a Christian, this is the truth about you. You *have* died to sin. Therefore, count on it; live in the light of it.

Count on It

Paul's vocabulary here comes from the world of accounting. What does an accountant do? He reckons; he counts; he calculates. Then he says to his client, "Here is the situation; these are your resources; this is what you can count on."

That is what Paul is saying. This is why he stresses that there are things we need to know. If we do not know them, we cannot count on them.

If you have not grasped the fact that through union with Jesus Christ you have died to the dominion of sin and been raised into newness of life, you will never count on it and you will never live in the light of it.

God says: "Dear child, don't you understand what I have done in drawing you to faith in my Son, the Lord Jesus? In Him you have died to the old life and been raised to the new life. You have died to sin—it no longer has dominion over you. Count on it! Count yourself to be dead to sin but alive to God in Christ Jesus."

You are now in a position to refuse to let sin reign in your mortal body and make you obey its evil desires (v. 12). You are able to resist the pressure you still feel from indwelling sin. You can say: "I know you are there; I feel your influence and sense your presence, but I am no longer under your authority. Therefore, I am not going to let you reign. By God's grace, I have been delivered from your dominion, and I am determined to live as one who is under the dominion of my Lord Jesus Christ."

This is what leads Paul to his exhortation: "Do not present your members as instruments of unrighteousness to sin, but present yourselves to God as being alive from the dead, and your members as instruments of God to righteousness" (v. 13).

Here, then, is how I am to think about myself:

Who am I?

• I have been raised into newness of life in Jesus Christ.

• I am no longer under sin's dominion.

What, then, am I to do with these instruments God has given to me?

• What am I prepared to listen to with my ears?

• What am I going to look at with my eyes?

• What am I going to do with my hands?

• What am I going to say with my tongue?

• What direction will I go with my feet?

Here is the response of the believer:

Take my life, and let it be consecrated, Lord, to Thee.
Take my moments and my days; let them flow in ceaseless praise.

Take my hands, and let them move at the impulse of Thy love.
Take my feet, and let them be swift and beautiful for Thee.

Take my voice, and let me sing always, only, for my King.
Take my lips, and let them be filled with messages from Thee.

Take my love, my Lord, I pour at Thy feet its treasure store.
Take myself, and I will be ever, only, all for Thee.[38]

I am going to offer all that I am—my eyes, my ears, my hands, my tongue, my feet—to my Lord Jesus Christ. Then the reign of His grace established in my life will overflow as I serve Him for His glory.

This, then, is the truth: "For sin shall not have dominion over you, because you are not under law but under grace" (v. 14).

I live already in the new world of grace. I no longer live in Sin Dominion, but in Grace Dominion. I am free at last.

That is the meaning of the last verse in Pastor Sibomana's hymn:

Praise him who broke the chain
Holding me in sin's domain
And set me free again!
Sing and rejoice!

It echoes the words of a much earlier hymn:

Be of sin the double cure.
Cleanse me from its guilt and power.[39]

Have you begun to experience "the double cure"? It is found in the pardon of the guilt of sin and the breaking of the power of sin. Both of these are ours through faith in Jesus Christ. And they are ours by grace alone.

That is the grace of God. When you discover it, it is absolutely amazing. It makes you want to sing:

"O how the grace of God amazes me!"

NOTES

1   From the hymn "Amazing Grace!" by John Newton, 1779.

2   From the hymn "When I Survey the Wondrous Cross" by Isaac Watts, 1707.

3   From the hymn "And Can It Be That I Should Gain" by Charles Wesley, 1738.

4   From the hymn "I Stand Amazed in the Presence" by Charles H. Gabriel, 1905.

5   William Law, *A Serious Call to a Devout and Holy Life*, was first published in 1728 and became a basic text for the group of friends who, with John and Charles Wesley, formed what was known as "The Holy Club." The group included George Whitefield, who had heard of their reputation even before he went to the University of Oxford.

6   From the hymn "And Can It Be That I Should Gain."

7   Ibid.

8   From the song "Dedicated Follower of Fashion" by Ray Davies and Raymond Douglas, 1966.

9   From the hymn "And Can It Be That I Should Gain."

10 Ibid.

11 Robert Burns, *Tam O'Shanter: A Tale*.

12 From the song "(I Can't Get No) Satisfaction" by Mick Jagger and Keith Richards, 1965.

13 See Kenneth Bailey, *The Cross and the Prodigal*, revised version (Downers Grove, Ill.: Inter-Varsity, 2005), 66ff. Perhaps no single author has done as much as Dr. Bailey to illumine the way in which a first-century Palestinian would have "heard" the parable of the prodigal son. In addition to the above, his reflections in *Poet and Peasant* (1976) and *Through Peasant Eyes* (1980), combined edition (Grand Rapids: Eerdmans, 1983), *Finding the Lost: Cultural Keys to Luke 15* (St. Louis: Concordia, 1992), and *Jacob and the Prodigal* (Downers Grove, Ill.: InterVarsity, 2003) make for illuminating and gripping reading.

14 Kenneth E Bailey, *Poet and Peasant* (Grand Rapids: Eerdmans, 1976), 181.

15 From the hymn, "Amazing Grace!"

16 He has told the story in *Pride and Perjury* (New York: HarperCollins, 2000).

17 From the hymn "There Is a Fountain Filled with Blood" by William Cowper, 1771.

18 From the hymn "How Deep the Father's Love For Us" by Stuart Townend, 1995.

19 From the hymn "Man of Sorrows! What a Name" by Philip Bliss, 1875.

20 From the hymn "He Stood before the Court" by Christopher Idle, 1982.

21 Christopher Lasch, *The Culture of Narcissism* (New York: W. W. Norton & Co., 1979). Narcissus was a figure in Greek mythology who fell in love with his reflection as he gazed into a river.

22 From J. H. Newman's poem, *The Dream of Gerontius*, 1865.

23 From the hymn "Man of Sorrows! What a Name."

24 From the hymn "Loved with Everlasting Love" by George Wade Robinson, 1890.

25 John Bunyan, *The Pilgrim's Progress* (originally published in 1678), ed. Roger Sharrock (Harmondsworth: Penguin, 1965), 57.

26 John Bunyan, *Grace Abounding to the Chief of Sinners*, in *The Works of John Bunyan*, ed. G. Offor (Glasgow, 1854), 1:18.

27 John Bunyan, *The Pilgrim's Progress* (originally published in 1678), ed. Roger Sharrock (Harmondsworth: Penguin, 1965), 57.

28 From the hymn "Approach, My Soul, the Mercy Seat" by John Newton, 1779.

29 Benjamin B. Warfield, *Biblical Doctrines* (1929; repr., Edinburgh: Banner of Truth, 1988), 504.

30 From the hymn "Before the Throne of God Above" by Charitie Bancroft, 1863.

31 John Calvin, *Institutes of the Christian Religion*, trans. Henry Beveridge (Peabody, Mass.: Hendrickson, 2008), 136.

32 From the hymn "My Faith Has Found a Resting Place" by Lidie H. Edmunds, 1891.

33 John Owen, *A Treatise of the Dominion of Sin and Grace* (1688), in *The Works of John Owen*, ed. William Goold (Edinburgh: Banner of Truth, 2001), 7:517.

34 Newman, *The Dream of Gerontius*.

35 From a Christian paraphrase of Psalm 72, "Jesus Shall Reign," by Isaac Watts, 1719.

36 J. B. Phillips, *The New Testament in Modern English* (London: Geoffrey Bles, 1960), 323.

37 From the hymn "Take My Life and Let It Be" by Frances R. Havergal, 1874.

38 Ibid.

39 From the hymn "Rock of Ages, Cleft for Me" by Augustus M. Toplady, 1776.

INDEX OF SCRIPTURE

ABOUT THE AUTHOR

Dr. Sinclair B. Ferguson is senior minister of the historical First Presbyterian Church in Columbia, S.C. He also serves as a professor of systematic theology at Redeemer Theological Seminary in Dallas, Texas, as a visiting professor in the doctor of ministry program at the Ligonier Academy of Biblical and Theological Studies, and as a teaching fellow of Ligonier Ministries.

A native of Scotland, Dr. Ferguson has earned three degrees, including his PhD, from the University of Aberdeen. He was ordained in the Church of Scotland and spent some sixteen years in ministry in his homeland, serving especially in St. George's-Tron Church in Glasgow. From 1983 to 1998, he served on the faculty of Westminster Theological Seminary in Philadelphia.

He is a trustee of the Banner of Truth Trust publishing house and is a member of the council of the Alliance of Confessing Evangelicals.

He is a prolific author. His published titles include *The Holy Spirit, Grow in Grace, Let's Study Philippians, John Owen on the Christian Life, In Christ Alone: Living the Gospel-Centered Life*, and, for children, *The Big Book of Questions & Answers* and *The Big Book of Questions & Answers About Jesus*.

Dr. Ferguson and his wife Dorothy have four children.